An Historical Survey of the

SOMERSET AND DORSET RAILWAY

TRACK LAYOUTS AND ILLUSTRATIONS

Frontispiece   An aerial view of Highbridge showing the S & D station in right foreground with the line to Burnham curving away in the middle distance. The GWR main line crosses the scene from left to right.

Aerofilms

An Historical Survey of the

SOMERSET AND DORSET RAILWAY

TRACK LAYOUTS AND ILLUSTRATIONS

by

C.W. Judge and C.R. Potts

Oxford Publishing Co.

Introduction

Having travelled over the Somerset and Dorset on several occasions in the late 50's, while in the Royal Air Force, I was aware of both the charming and tortuous terrain the "Slow and Dirty" encountered on its cross country route. Hills, cuttings, tunnels, gradients, embankments and tight curves were all a part of this railway's make up and in this book I have tried to include as many photographs and plans (both signalling and ground surveys) as possible to help you capture the character of the railway itself.

The idea for this work came mainly through my close friendship with the Somerset and Dorset's "own photographer", Ivo Peters, whose book "The Somerset and Dorset. An English Cross Country Railway" must be the finest tribute any person has paid to any English Railway. It is said that Ivo has photographed nearly every "sleeper" on the S & D. While working with him on his book, I was privileged to see the magnificent 16mm. colour films he had painstakingly compiled on this railway in the 60's. To be riding on the bankers; to watch the overflow traffic on the Summer Saturdays; to be on board, grinding up the Summits, coping with the snow drifts and watching the famous "Pines Express"; passing through places with enchanting names such as Horsecombe Vale, Tucking Mill, Midsomer Norton, Binegar, Holes Bay, Templecombe, Evercreech, Charlton Marshall, Corfe Mullen and many more; all this was the Somerset and Dorset.

After stumbling upon all the signalling plans about two years ago, I was prompted to prepare a more detailed thesis on this railway purely for my own enjoyment. As more material became available from friends such as Colin French, Dick Riley, Joe Moss, Peter Smith, John Smith, Ralph Clark and the Somerset and Dorset Railway Museum Trust it became obvious a serious attempt should be made to place this on paper. When finally the whole survey of the line (carried out by the Midland Railway in 1921) came into my possession the story was complete and a book was born. So many people up to this period in time had helped me but now my co-author Chris Potts stepped in and devoted many, many hours poring over reference books, old maps, manuscripts and timetables to make the textual matter as accurate as possible in the space we had available.

So there we are; born in 1862 as a result of the amalgamation of the Somerset Central Railway and the Dorset Central Railway, its main aim being a cross country link between the thriving Bristol Channel and the English Channel, the Somerset and Dorset Railway lasted just 104 glorious years, until 1966. Carrying so many holiday makers, business men, stone from the Mendips and freight, perhaps, in many eyes it should still be there, but alas it is no longer so I hope this book will, in a small way, help you "travel" and "enjoy" the SOMERSET AND DORSET RAILWAY.

Authors' Note

We have tried to compile a complete collection of track plans, photographs and notes on this famous railway, but would point out that records are sometimes vague and in some cases, non-existent. Many of the track plans and signal diagrams are of different scales, dates and even direction but we have included them in this state to try and portray a more complete survey of the line. Please note that the "plan dates" refer to the track plans. We would appreciate information from readers, which will be sent to the S&D Railway Museum Trust for inclusion in their records. We hope you enjoy our efforts.

Colin Judge Chris Potts
January 1979

Acknowledgements

We wish to acknowledge the help afforded to us by members of the Somerset and Dorset Railway Museum Trust. The information, plans and photographs contributed by them is the result of research of their own bi-monthly Bulletin which itself is a valuable record of historical material.

The present Trust started as the S&D Railway Circle in 1966 with the primary aim of collating and circulating information on the S&DJR. In 1969 practical preservation activities started and the station at Radstock North was leased as a base. The decision to acquire S&DJR 2-8-0 locomotive No. 88 located at Barry was taken, and after extensive preliminary restoration the engine moved by rail to Radstock in the autumn of 1970. In 1973 the S&DRMT was formed to regulate the growing complexities of running trains at Radstock on the S&D line to Writhlington Colliery, and to benefit from charitable status. In early 1974 it was realised that the Radstock project was liable to fail and the search for a new site led the Trust to the West Somerset Railway. After cordial negotiations with the West Somerset Railway Company, Washford was mutually agreed upon as the most suitable site for the now extensive collection of locomotives and rolling stock.

In May 1975 the move from Radstock began with the transport of various industrial locomotives and wagons and the move to the W.S.R. was finally completed in January 1976 with the arrival of No. 88 together with two coaches and a G.W. toad brake van. Following an access point being installed at Washford in August 1976 the siding area has been steadily increased until in December 1977 the last item of stock, 2-8-0 No. 88 finally arrived on site. Work continues to extend the sidings, build a locomotive shed with a pit and workshop, and to restore the stock in the Trust's care to working order and ensure that one of the most interesting and best loved railways in Great Britain, the Somerset and Dorset Joint Railway, will always be remembered.

Also grateful thanks are due to Ralph Clark for checking the manuscript and supplying some valuable information, also tabulating the opening and closing dates; the Signalling Record Society for supplying nearly all the signalling plans and the Southern Railway Group for information regarding S & D signal boxes.

For the supply of photographs our thanks go to the following:
Aerofilms, Robin Atthill, British Rail, Ralph Clark, G.R. Hounsell, W. Vaughan-Jenkins, G. Judd, Lens of Sutton, L.G.R.P., W. Locke, M. Malden, D. Milton, National Railway Museum, Dr. Michael O'Connor, H.B. Oliver, M.J. Palmer, Pamlin Prints, Photomatic, George Pryer, G.W. Puntis, Dick Riley, Bernard Robinson, A.L. Rush, South Devon Railway Museum.

And a final word of thanks for the person without whom the Printer's job would be a difficult one; Chris's wife, Sue, for her diligent typing and re-typing of the manuscript.

Printed by Blackwell's in the City of Oxford

Published by the
Oxford Railway Publishing Co. Ltd
8 The Roundway
Headington, Oxford

Winsor Hill signal box 'framed' by the north portal of the New Tunnel. *R.H. Clark*

Bibliography

The Somerset & Dorset Railway *by Robin Atthill* (David & Charles)
The Somerset & Dorset: An English Cross Country Railway *by Ivo Peters* (Oxford Publishing Company)
Track Layout Diagrams section 18, S & D Railway, *by R. A. Cooke* and published by the author.
The Picture History of the Somerset and Dorset Railway *by Robin Atthill* (David & Charles)
The Somerset & Dorset Railway *by D.S. Barrie and C.R. Clinker* (Oakwood Press Ltd)
Highbridge in its Heyday *by Colin Maggs* (Oakwood Press Ltd)
Working Timetables 1920 and 1930 (Reprint) Oxford Publishing Co. Ltd

Key to Symbols

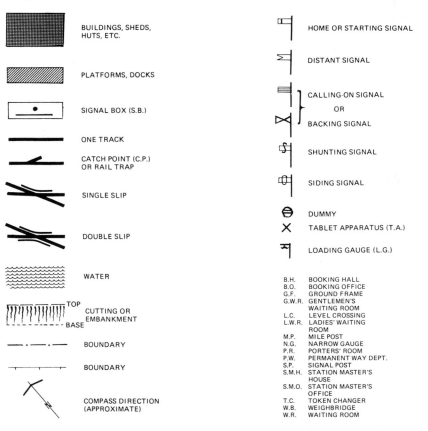

BUILDINGS, SHEDS, HUTS, ETC.

PLATFORMS, DOCKS

SIGNAL BOX (S.B.)

ONE TRACK

CATCH POINT (C.P.) OR RAIL TRAP

SINGLE SLIP

DOUBLE SLIP

WATER

CUTTING OR EMBANKMENT — TOP / BASE

BOUNDARY

BOUNDARY

COMPASS DIRECTION (APPROXIMATE)

HOME OR STARTING SIGNAL

DISTANT SIGNAL

CALLING-ON SIGNAL OR BACKING SIGNAL

SHUNTING SIGNAL

SIDING SIGNAL

DUMMY

TABLET APPARATUS (T.A.)

LOADING GAUGE (L.G.)

B.H.   BOOKING HALL
B.O.   BOOKING OFFICE
G.F.   GROUND FRAME
G.W.R. GENTLEMEN'S WAITING ROOM
L.C.   LEVEL CROSSING
L.W.R. LADIES' WAITING ROOM
M.P.   MILE POST
N.G.   NARROW GAUGE
P.R.   PORTERS' ROOM
P.W.   PERMANENT WAY DEPT.
S.P.   SIGNAL POST
S.M.H. STATION MASTER'S HOUSE
S.M.O. STATION MASTER'S OFFICE
T.C.   TOKEN CHANGER
W.B.   WEIGHBRIDGE
W.R.   WAITING ROOM

THE SOMERSET and DORSET JOINT RAILWAY

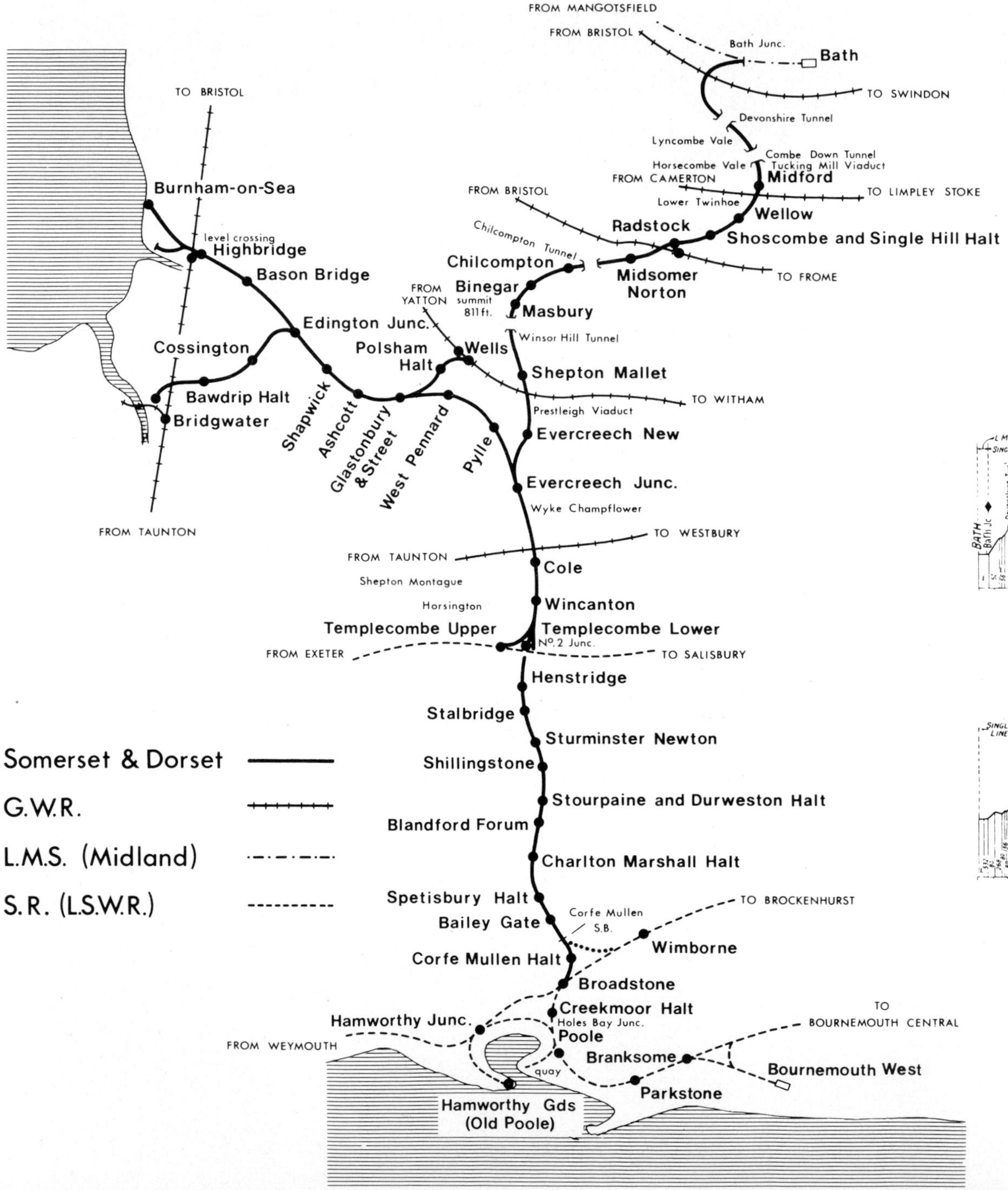

FROM MANGOTSFIELD
FROM BRISTOL
Bath Junc.
Bath
TO SWINDON
TO BRISTOL
Devonshire Tunnel
Lyncombe Vale
Combe Down Tunnel
Horsecombe Vale
Tucking Mill Viaduct
FROM CAMERTON
Midford
TO LIMPLEY STOKE
FROM BRISTOL
Lower Twinhoe
Wellow
Burnham-on-Sea
Radstock
Shoscombe and Single Hill Halt
level crossing
Highbridge
Chilcompton Tunnel
Chilcompton
Midsomer Norton
TO FROME
Bason Bridge
FROM YATTON
Binegar
summit 811 ft.
Masbury
Edington Junc.
Winsor Hill Tunnel
Cossington
Polsham Halt
Wells
Shepton Mallet
Bawdrip Halt
TO WITHAM
Bridgwater
Prestleigh Viaduct
Shapwick
Ashcott
Glastonbury & Street
West Pennard
Pylle
Evercreech New
Evercreech Junc.
Wyke Champflower
FROM TAUNTON
TO WESTBURY
FROM TAUNTON
Cole
Shepton Montague
Horsington
Wincanton
Templecombe Upper
Templecombe Lower
No. 2 Junc.
FROM EXETER
TO SALISBURY
Henstridge
Stalbridge
Sturminster Newton
Shillingstone
Somerset & Dorset
G.W.R.
L.M.S. (Midland)
S.R. (L.S.W.R.)
Stourpaine and Durweston Halt
Blandford Forum
Charlton Marshall Halt
Spetisbury Halt
TO BROCKENHURST
Corfe Mullen S.B.
Bailey Gate
Wimborne
Corfe Mullen Halt
Broadstone
Creekmoor Halt
TO BOURNEMOUTH CENTRAL
Hamworthy Junc.
Holes Bay Junc.
Poole
FROM WEYMOUTH
Branksome
quay
Bournemouth West
Parkstone
Hamworthy Gds (Old Poole)

BATH
Bath Jc
L M S
SINGLE LINE
Devonshire Tunl
Combe Down Tunnel
MIDFORD
WELLOW
RADSTOCK
MIDSOMER NORTON
Tunnel
CHILCOMPTON
Moorewood Sdg
BINEGAR
MASBURY
Winsor Hill Tunl
Downside Sdg
SHEPTON MALLET
EVERCREECH (NEW)
Jc with Burnham Line
EVERCREECH JC
COLE
WINCANTON
No 3 Jc
No 2 Jc
Lower Stn
Templecombe
TEMPLECOMBE JUNCT
HENSTRIDGE
STALBRIDGE
SINGLE LINE
STURMINSTER NEWTON
SHILLINGSTONE
20
30
40
50 M

BATH—BOURNEMOUTH WEST

SINGLE LINE
BLANDFORD
SPETISBURY
BAILEY GATE
Corfe Mullen Jc
SINGLE LINE
S. RY
BROADSTONE
Holes Bay Jc
POOLE
PARKSTONE
BRANKSOME
Bournemouth W Jc
BOURNEMOUTH W.
60
70 M

BATH—BOURNEMOUTH WEST

SINGLE LINE MAXIMUM SPEED 45 M P H
EVERCREECH JC
Jc with Main Line
PYLLE
WEST PENNARD
GLASTONBURY
ASHCOTT
SHAPWICK
EDINGTON JC
BASON BRIDGE
HIGHBRIDGE
BURNHAM
24

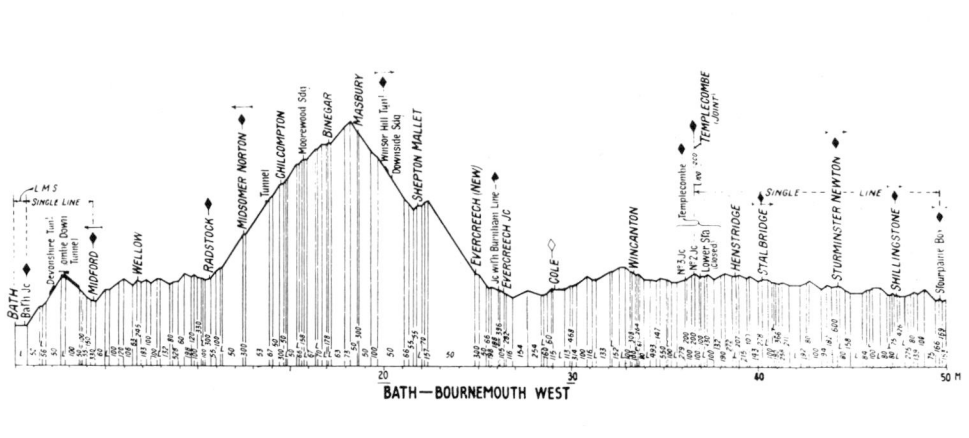

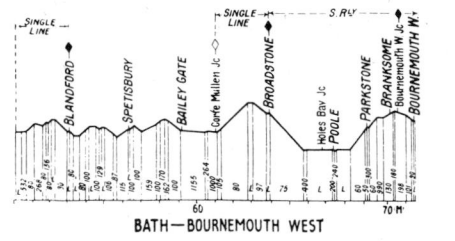

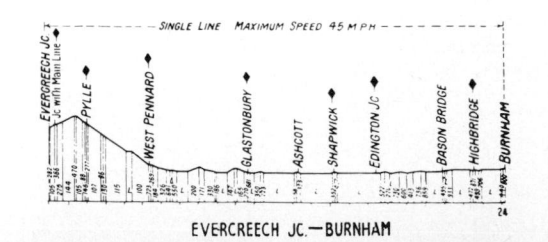

EVERCREECH JC.—BURNHAM

gradient profiles by permission of The Railway Magazine.

Bath to Broadstone and Wimborne

BATH GREEN PARK

Opened: 7 May 1870 (replaced former Midland temporary station)
20 July 1874 (used by S & D trains from this date)
Closed: 7 March 1966
Plan date: 1921

Opened in 1870, the Bath terminus was at that time at the end of the ten mile long branch of the Midland Railway from Mangotsfield. After the opening of the Bath extension of the S & D (from Evercreech Jc.) on 20th July, 1874, it was shared with the latter company. The station was renamed Bath Green Park on and from 18th June, 1951; in the intervening period it was known as Bath Queen Square in 'Bradshaw' but this was not an official title.

Bath Green Park was a four road station under an arched glass roof which ran for about half the length of the platform. Only two of the four lines had platform faces, the two centre roads being used for running round and coach stabling. Somerset and Dorset trains used either platform as available, although most of the through trains used the southern platform. Neither platform was adequate for the long summer express trains; the southern platform could only accommodate nine bogie coaches, the northern platform one less.

Bath Green Park   Down train being assembled, 1961.   *OPC Collection*

Bath Green Park   The buffer stops end.   *R.C. Riley*

Bath Green Park   Looking towards the country.   *Lens of Sutton*

7

Bath Green Park   The elegant façade of the station, seen here in 1959.   *R.H. Clark*

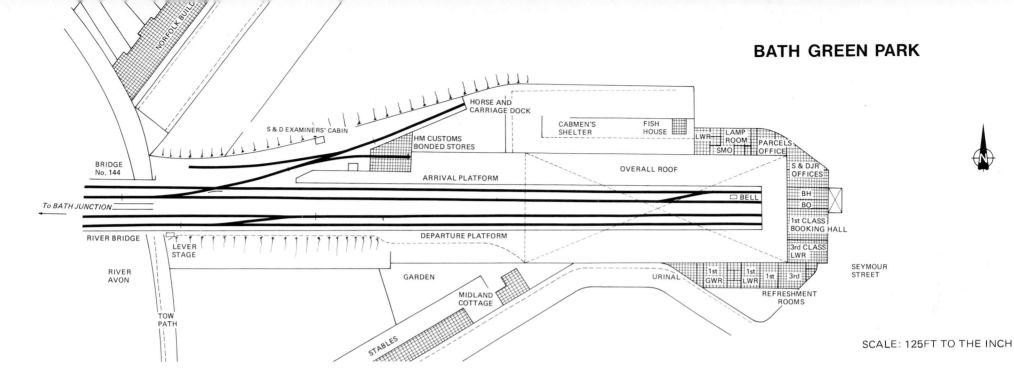

BATH GREEN PARK

NORFOLK BUILD...

HORSE AND CARRIAGE DOCK

S & D EXAMINERS' CABIN

HM CUSTOMS BONDED STORES

CABMEN'S SHELTER

FISH HOUSE

LWR

LAMP ROOM

SMO

PARCELS OFFICE

BRIDGE No. 144

OVERALL ROOF

ARRIVAL PLATFORM

S & DJR OFFICES

BH

BO

BELL

To BATH JUNCTION

1st CLASS BOOKING HALL

RIVER BRIDGE

DEPARTURE PLATFORM

3rd CLASS LWR

LEVER STAGE

SEYMOUR STREET

RIVER AVON

GARDEN

URINAL

1st GWR

1st LWR

1st

3rd

TOW PATH

MIDLAND COTTAGE

REFRESHMENT ROOMS

STABLES

SCALE: 125FT TO THE INCH

Bath Green Park The handsome Seymour Street frontage. *R.C. Riley*

Bath Green Park A 1959 view. *R.C. Riley*

Bath Green Park A view of the gloomy interior under the overall roof. *Lens of Sutton*

Bath Green Park The left hand platform line was classed as the arrival line and the right hand platform line the departure line, but they were both signalled in either direction.
OPC Collection

BATH STATION

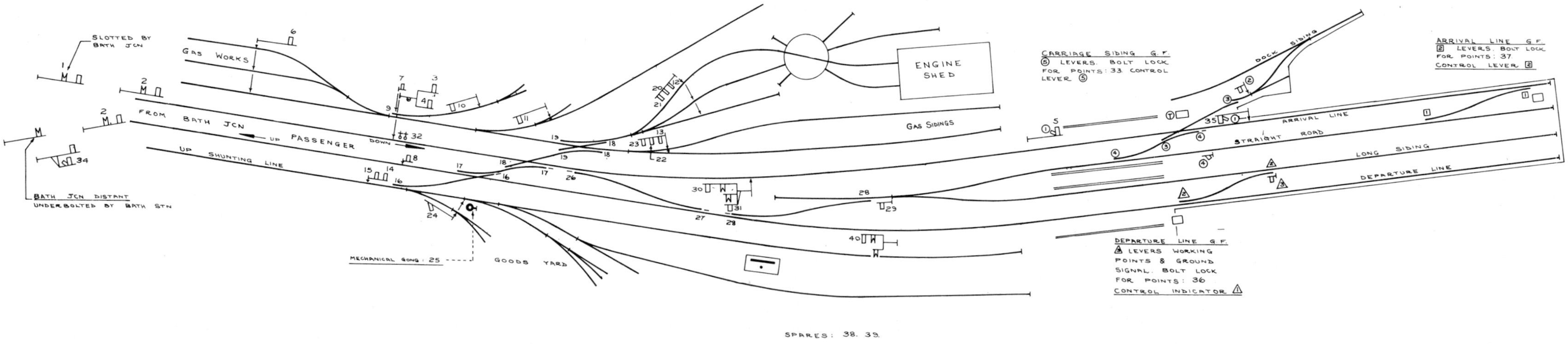

SLOTTED BY
BATH JCN
GAS WORKS

6

1 M

7 3

2 M

9

4

10

ARRIVAL LINE G.F.
8 LEVERS. BOLT LOCK
FOR POINTS. 37
CONTROL LEVER 8

CARRIAGE SIDING G.F.
5 LEVERS. BOLT LOCK
FOR POINTS. 33. CONTROL
LEVER 5

DOCK SIDING

ENGINE
SHED

2 FROM BATH JCN

UP PASSENGER

DOWN

32

11

29
21

20

13

18

13
23

GAS SIDINGS

5

T

35

ARRIVAL LINE

STRAIGHT ROAD

M

UP SHUNTING LINE

8

15 14

18

17
16

15
16

17
26

22

28

29

30
31

LONG SIDING

DEPARTURE LINE

34

BATH JCN DISTANT
UNDERBOLTED BY BATH STN

24

MECHANICAL GONG. 25

GOODS YARD

27 28

40

DEPARTURE LINE G.F.
4 LEVERS WORKING
POINTS & GROUND
SIGNAL. BOLT LOCK
FOR POINTS. 36
CONTROL INDICATOR

SPARES: 38. 39.

Bath Shed   LMS 4F 0-6-0 No. 44264 on the turntable at Bath shed on 2nd May, 1965.

G.R. Hounsell

BATH GREEN PARK

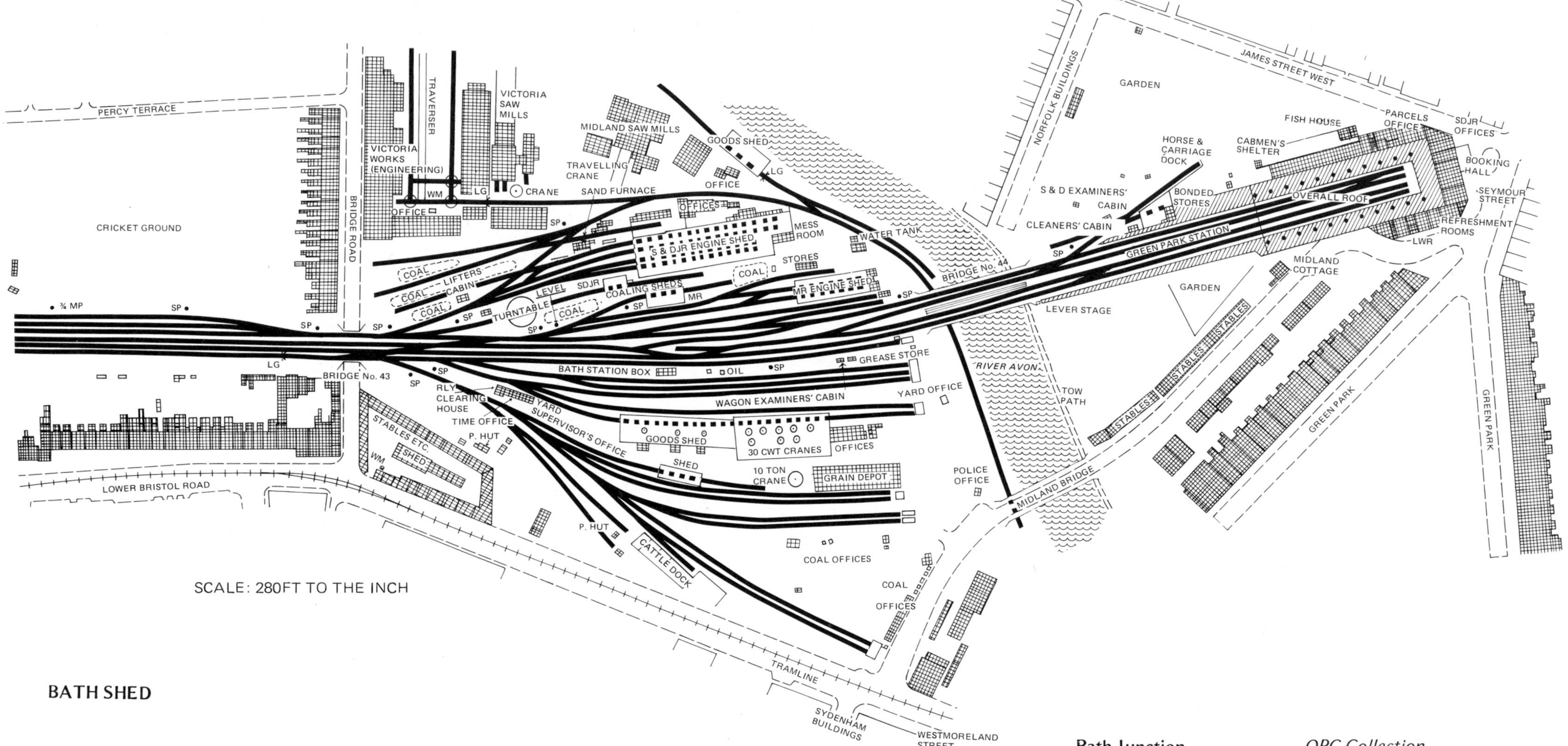

Map labels:

STANHOPE PLACE
JAMES STREET WEST
PERCY TERRACE
TRAVERSER
VICTORIA SAW MILLS
MIDLAND SAW MILLS
GOODS SHED
NORFOLK BUILDINGS
GARDEN
FISH HOUSE
PARCELS OFFICE
SDJR OFFICES
HORSE & CARRIAGE DOCK
CABMEN'S SHELTER
BOOKING HALL
VICTORIA WORKS (ENGINEERING)
TRAVELLING CRANE
OFFICE
LG
S & D EXAMINERS' CABIN
BONDED STORES
OVERALL ROOF
SEYMOUR STREET
WM
LG
CRANE
SAND FURNACE
OFFICES
MESS ROOM
WATER TANK
CLEANERS' CABIN
REFRESHMENT ROOMS
CRICKET GROUND
OFFICE
S & DJR ENGINE SHED
STORES
COAL
MR ENGINE SHED
BRIDGE No. 44
GREEN PARK STATION
LWR
COAL LIFTERS
COAL CABIN
SDJR
COALING SHEDS
MR
COAL
SP
LEVEL
TURNTABLE
COAL
LEVER STAGE
GARDEN
MIDLAND COTTAGE
BRIDGE ROAD
¾ MP
SP
SP
SP
SP
SP
SP
SP
BATH STATION BOX
OIL
SP
GREASE STORE
RIVER AVON
TOW PATH
STABLES
GREEN PARK
LG
BRIDGE No. 43
SP
SP
RLY CLEARING HOUSE
TIME OFFICE
YARD SUPERVISOR'S OFFICE
WAGON EXAMINERS' CABIN
YARD OFFICE
STABLES ETC.
P. HUT
WM
SHED
GOODS SHED
30 CWT CRANES
OFFICES
TOW
LOWER BRISTOL ROAD
SHED
10 TON CRANE
GRAIN DEPOT
POLICE OFFICE
MIDLAND BRIDGE
P. HUT
CATTLE DOCK
COAL OFFICES
COAL OFFICES
SCALE: 280FT TO THE INCH
TRAMLINE
SYDENHAM BUILDINGS
WESTMORELAND STREET

BATH SHED

Plan date: 1921

The S & D Motive Power Depot at Bath was a wooden structure and contained four roads. The shed was about 300 feet long by 60 feet wide. Alongside and at a higher level was the coal stage road and adjacent to it was a 60 foot turntable; this was shared by the S & D and the Midland sheds. The Midland shed was a stone built structure. In 1928 the control of both sheds came under the S & D locomotive superintendent and from 1930 the Midland shed tended to be used for engines undergoing extensive repair.

Bath Junction.   *OPC Collection*

Bath Shed   A busy scene in June 1962.   *R.C. Riley*

Bath Shed   Ex-LMS 2P 4-4-0 No. 40697.   *S. Devon Railway Museum*

Bath Shed   The ex-Midland stone built shed with 0-6-0 PTs Nos. 3758 and 3677.
S. Devon Railway Museum

Bath Shed   The ex-Midland shed in 1960.   *R.C. Riley*

Bath Junction The signal box and Bath Gasworks.

P.I. Clarke

Bath Junction On 14th May, 1960 BR 4-6-0 No. 75027 with the 11.04 am Bournemouth West to Bristol descends the 1 in 50 gradient at Bath Jc.

OPC Collection

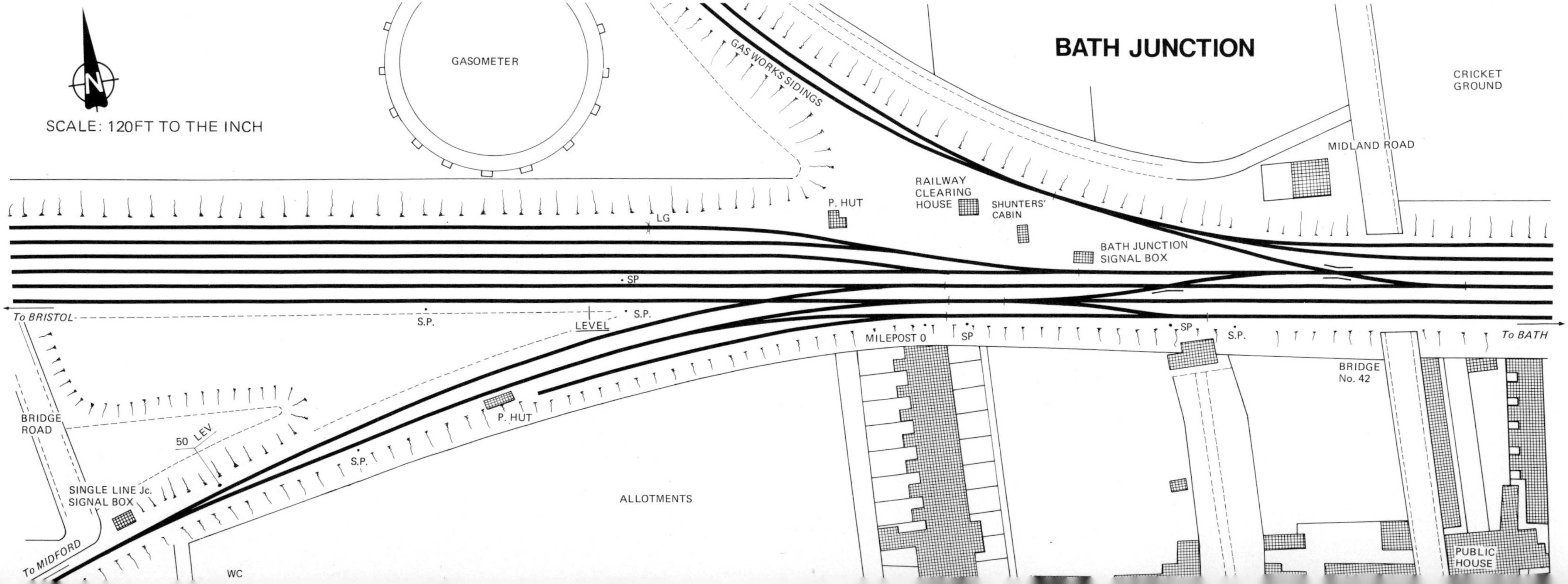

BATH JUNCTION

SCALE: 120FT TO THE INCH

GASOMETER

GAS WORKS SIDINGS

CRICKET GROUND

MIDLAND ROAD

RAILWAY CLEARING HOUSE

P. HUT

SHUNTERS' CABIN

BATH JUNCTION SIGNAL BOX

LG

SP

To BRISTOL

S.P.

LEVEL

S.P.

MILEPOST 0

SP

SP

S.P.

To BATH

BRIDGE No. 42

BRIDGE ROAD

50 LEV

P. HUT

S.P.

SINGLE LINE Jc. SIGNAL BOX

ALLOTMENTS

To MIDFORD

WC

PUBLIC HOUSE

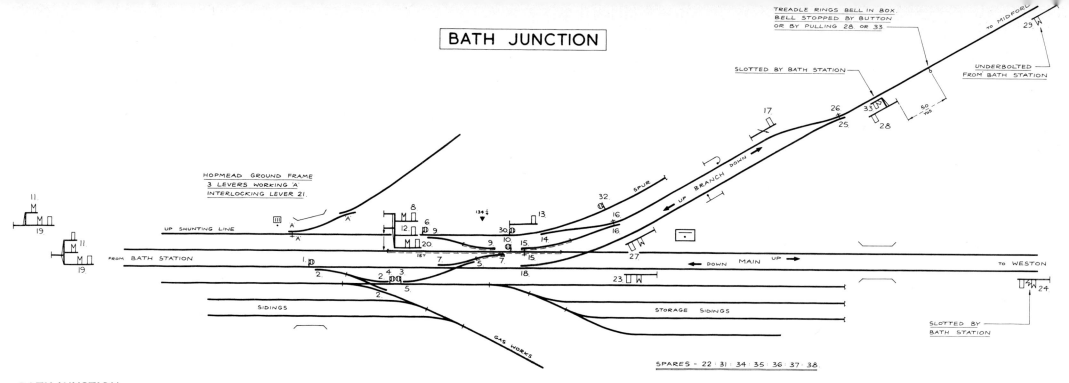

BATH JUNCTION

TREADLE RINGS BELL IN BOX.
BELL STOPPED BY BUTTON
OR BY PULLING 28 OR 33

TO MIDFORD

SLOTTED BY BATH STATION

UNDERBOLTED
FROM BATH STATION

HOPMEAD GROUND FRAME
3 LEVERS WORKING 'A'
INTERLOCKING LEVER 21.

UP SHUNTING LINE

FROM BATH STATION

SIDINGS

GAS WORKS

SPUR

UP BRANCH DOWN

DOWN MAIN UP

TO WESTON

STORAGE SIDINGS

SLOTTED BY
BATH STATION

SPARES — 22 : 31 : 34 : 35 : 36 : 37 : 38.

BATH JUNCTION

Plan date: 1921

The box was 41 chains from Green Park Station and marked the start of the S & D proper. The layout above is that of the second Bath Junction box opened on 13th April, 1924. Before this date there had been an additional box where the double track of the S & D section became single, called Bath Single Line Junction Box; this had been less than one hundred yards from Bath Junction.

Bath Junction was at the foot of a 1 in 50 incline to Combe Down tunnel, about two miles away. Bank engines were provided at the rear of down freight trains and these assisted without being coupled to the train. The driver of the train engine picked up the tablet for the single line section to Midford at Bath Jc., whilst the driver of the bank engine was issued with a special 'Bath bank engine staff'. Having banked the freight train into Combe Down tunnel, this staff was the driver's authority to return to Bath Jc. box, thirteen minutes being allowed for the complete journey. The bank engine also performed shunting duties at the two intermediate sidings (Twerton Co-op and Victoria Brick & Tile), the ground frames being released by the bank engine staff.

Bath Junction The down 'Pines Express' swings over Bath Jc. and heads for Bournemouth on 14th May, 1960. 4-4-0 No. 40634 and 4-6-0 No. 73052 provide the power.

OPC Collection

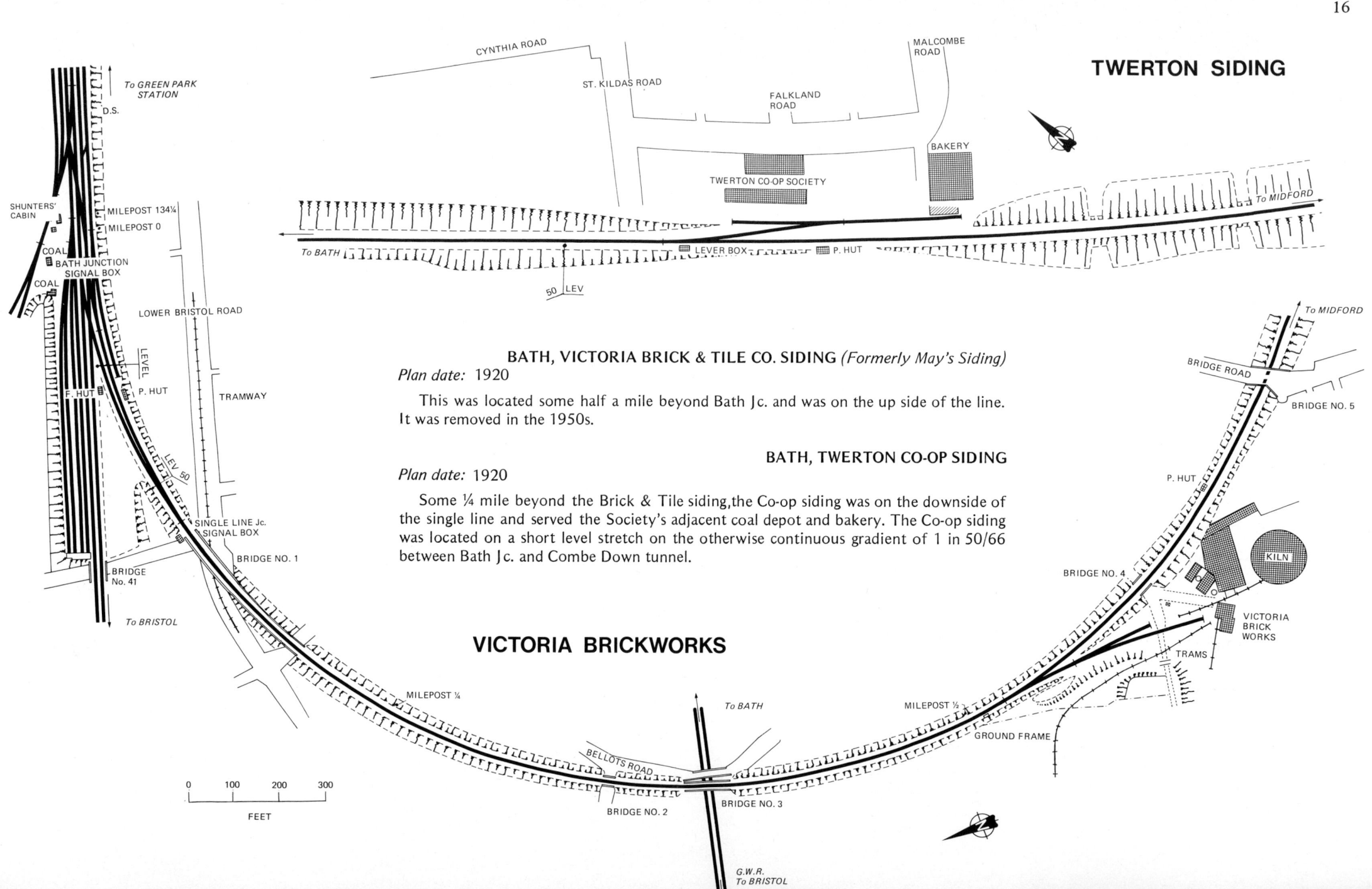

TWERTON SIDING

CYNTHIA ROAD

ST. KILDAS ROAD

MALCOMBE ROAD

FALKLAND ROAD

BAKERY

TWERTON CO-OP SOCIETY

To MIDFORD

To BATH

LEVER BOX

P. HUT

50 LEV

To GREEN PARK STATION

D.S.

SHUNTERS' CABIN

MILEPOST 134¼

MILEPOST 0

COAL

BATH JUNCTION SIGNAL BOX

COAL

LOWER BRISTOL ROAD

LEVEL

P. HUT

F. HUT

TRAMWAY

LEV 50

SINGLE LINE Jc. SIGNAL BOX

BRIDGE NO. 1

BRIDGE No. 41

To BRISTOL

To MIDFORD

BRIDGE ROAD

BRIDGE NO. 5

P. HUT

KILN

BRIDGE NO. 4

VICTORIA BRICK WORKS

TRAMS

GROUND FRAME

BATH, VICTORIA BRICK & TILE CO. SIDING (*Formerly May's Siding*)

Plan date: 1920

This was located some half a mile beyond Bath Jc. and was on the up side of the line. It was removed in the 1950s.

BATH, TWERTON CO-OP SIDING

Plan date: 1920

Some ¼ mile beyond the Brick & Tile siding, the Co-op siding was on the downside of the single line and served the Society's adjacent coal depot and bakery. The Co-op siding was located on a short level stretch on the otherwise continuous gradient of 1 in 50/66 between Bath Jc. and Combe Down tunnel.

VICTORIA BRICKWORKS

MILEPOST ¼

To BATH

MILEPOST ½

BELLOTS ROAD

BRIDGE NO. 2

BRIDGE NO. 3

G.W.R. To BRISTOL

0   100   200   300

FEET

MIDFORD

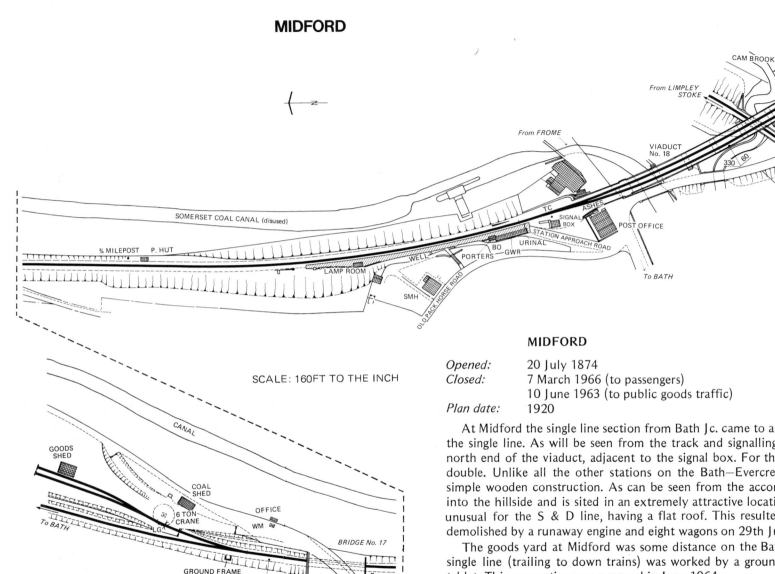

SCALE: 160FT TO THE INCH

MIDFORD

Opened:	20 July 1874
Closed:	7 March 1966 (to passengers)
	10 June 1963 (to public goods traffic)
Plan date:	1920

At Midford the single line section from Bath Jc. came to an end, although the station itself was located on the single line. As will be seen from the track and signalling plan the double line originally started at the north end of the viaduct, adjacent to the signal box. For the next 32 miles to Templecombe the track was double. Unlike all the other stations on the Bath—Evercreech section the buildings at Midford were of simple wooden construction. As can be seen from the accompanying photographs the station is built right into the hillside and is sited in an extremely attractive location. The sixteen lever signal box was somewhat unusual for the S & D line, having a flat roof. This resulted from its reconstruction after being partially demolished by a runaway engine and eight wagons on 29th July, 1936.

The goods yard at Midford was some distance on the Bath side of the station and the connection in the single line (trailing to down trains) was worked by a ground frame (Midford 'A') released by the section tablet. This connection was removed in June 1964.

The tall latticed post signal midway along the platform was a Backing signal. If an up train stalled on the severe gradient between Midford and Combe Down tunnel, the Driver would use the telephone adjacent to the tunnel to obtain permission from the Midford signalman to set back to the latter station. The Backing signals would be pulled off and the train reversed onto the up line on Midford viaduct until assistance was available.

Midford   A view towards Bath showing the small goods yard on right.   *OPC collection*

Midford   A view over the goods yard buffer stops towards Bath.   *OPC collection*

Midford   Looking down the bank towards Midford station; points from goods yard in foreground. Note backing signal as lower arm to down home signal.   *OPC collection*

Midford   Looking towards Wellow; the line became double midway over the viaduct.
Lens of Sutton

Midford A close-up of the tall backing signal on the platform.
OPC collection

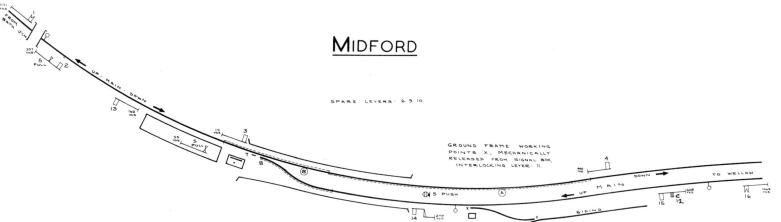

MIDFORD

SPARE LEVERS: 6. 9. 10.

GROUND FRAME WORKING
POINTS 'X'. MECHANICALLY
RELEASED FROM SIGNAL BOX.
INTERLOCKING LEVER: 11.

Midford The flat roofed signal box with station beyond.
R.C. Riley

Midford A view over the viaduct towards Wellow showing double line junction.
OPC collection

WELLOW

Opened: 20 July 1874
Closed: 7 March 1966 (to passengers)
10 June 1963 (to goods)
The sidings and crossover at the south end of the station were taken out on 30 June 1964.
Plan date: 1921

Some 6¾ miles from Bath Green Park the small station of Wellow was reached. This station was always well used because buses reached the village only once a week. The station building was a compact structure built in grey limestone with a slate roof and comprised of: station master's office, combined booking hall and waiting room and a ladies room. Also located on the up platform was a small stone built store room and a small metal shed which was used as a lamp room. On the opposite down platform there was solely a small wooden hut.

The attractive signal box of eighteen levers stood at the eastern end of the down platform. A block switch was provided at this box.

Wellow   The station building.   *OPC collection*

WELLOW

SCALE: 120FT TO THE INCH

WELLOW

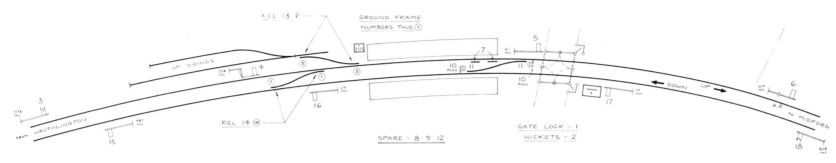

REL 13 2

GROUND FRAME
NUMBERS THUS ①

UP SIDINGS

FROM WRITHLINGTON

REL 14 ①

SPARE - 8 9 12

GATE LOCK - 1
WICKETS - 2

DOWN   UP

A 8   TO MIDFORD

Wellow   Looking towards Midford.

Lens of Sutton

Wellow   The small goods yard.

OPC collection

21

Shoscombe & Single Hill Halt   Looking towards Radstock.   *Lens of Sutton*

Opened: 23 September 1929
Closed: 7 March 1966
Plan date: c. 1930's

This was a simple two platform halt opened on 23rd September, 1929. The two platforms were built in concrete and were devoid of any buildings. A small booking office and waiting room was provided beside the footpath leading up to the village.

SHOSCOMBE & SINGLE HILL HALT

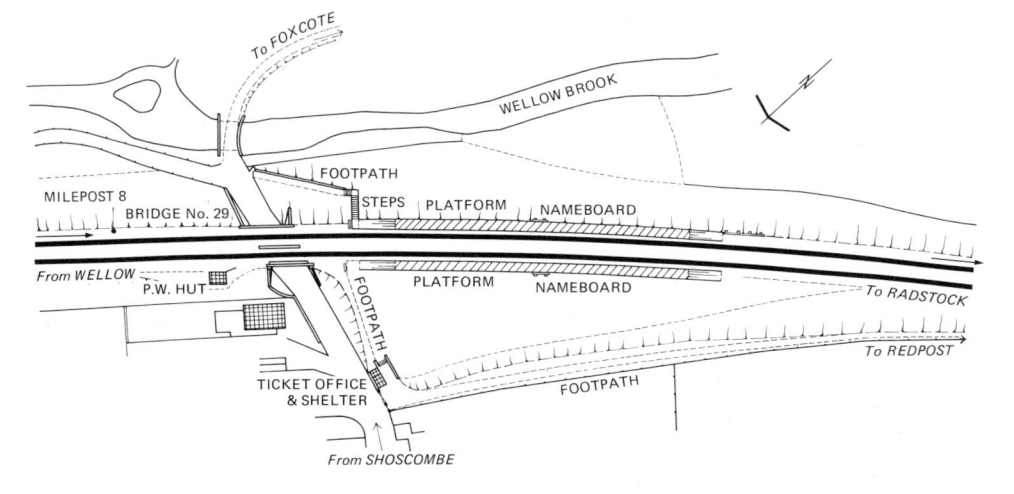

WRITHLINGTON

Plan date: 1921

The signal box here, which controlled access to the sidings serving Lower Writhlington and Braysdown collieries was opened in May 1875 and at that time was known as Foxcote. On 7th August, 1876 it was the scene of a hideous head-on collision — the track at that time being single line — between an up relief train and a down excursion, it being Bank Holiday Monday. The crash, which is fully described in Robin Atthill's book 'The Somerset & Dorset Railway' (David & Charles), was due to a signalling irregularity (not caused by the Foxcote signalman) and led to the death of twelve passengers and the excursion train guard. All the passengers came from Radstock to which the excursion was returning and the grief of that village can be imagined.

A new signal box was opened at Writhlington in July 1894.

After closure of the Somerset and Dorset line in March 1966, the coal from Writhlington was taken down the old S & D line to Radstock where a new connection had been laid in giving access to the Western Region Bristol—Frome line. After closure of the section between Radstock and Bristol in 1968, a circuitous journey was made via Frome and Westbury before Bristol was gained.

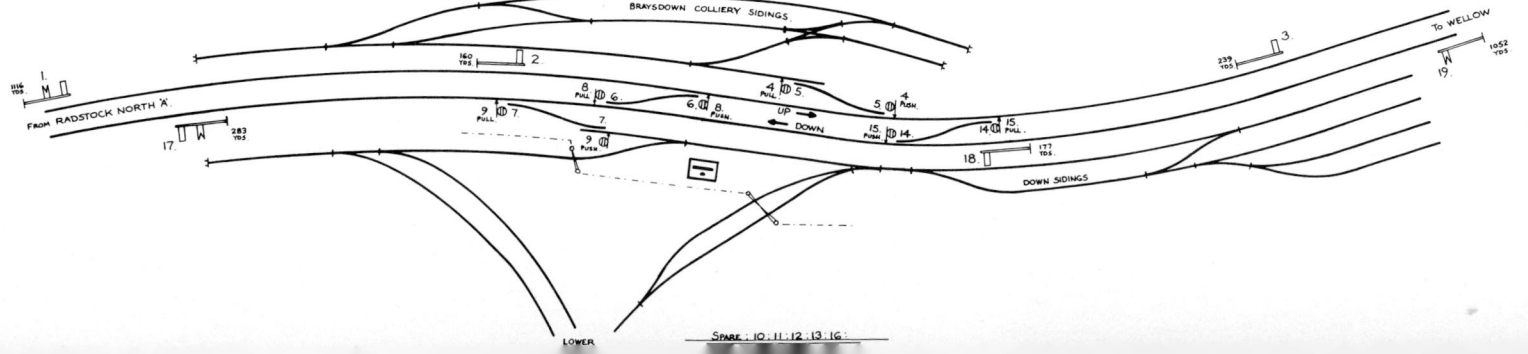

WRITHLINGTON

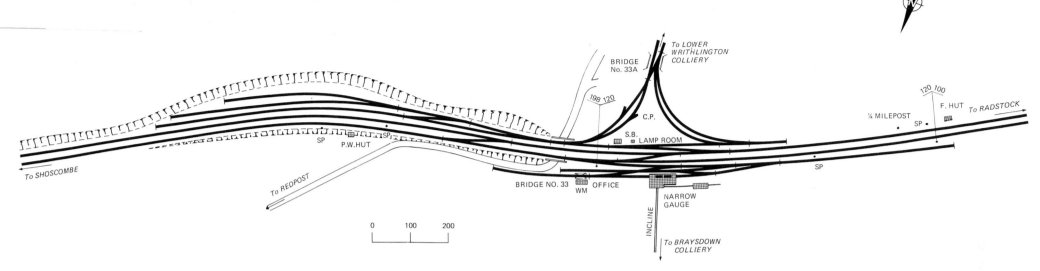

To LOWER WRITHLINGTON COLLIERY

BRIDGE No. 33A

198 120

C.P.

120 100

¼ MILEPOST

SP

F. HUT

To RADSTOCK

S.B.

LAMP ROOM

SP

SP

To SHOSCOMBE

SP

P.W. HUT

SP

To REDPOST

BRIDGE NO. 33

WM

OFFICE

NARROW GAUGE

INCLINE

To BRAYSDOWN COLLIERY

SP

0   100   200

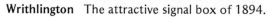

Writhlington The attractive signal box of 1894.

P.I. Clarke

Writhlington The signal box and colliery c. 1900.

British Rail

S.&D. STATION. RADSTOCK. 1106.

Radstock   An early view of the station and staff.   *OPC Collection*

Opened:	20 July 1874
Closed:	7 March 1966 (to passengers)
	15 June 1964 (to public goods traffic)
Renaming:	'Radstock' until 26 September 1949
Plan date:	1921

The S & D station at Radstock North was immediately adjacent to the GWR station — Radstock South — but no physical connection for through traffic between them existed until closure of the S & D in 1966, when a connection south of the station was put in for the coal traffic from Writhlington to Portishead. The layout was quite extensive, as may be seen from the plans, and controlled from two signal boxes. These were originally known as Radstock East and West but were renamed Radstock North 'A' and North 'B' respectively in 1951. The level crossing controlled by North 'B' signal box was close to a similar level crossing at the adjacent GWR station, and, between them, they could cause miles of road traffic jams in the summer months!

The small two road stone built engine shed housed the bank engines that were required to bank practically all down freight trains over the 7½ miles to Masbury summit, the gradient for much of the distance being 1 in 50. In addition the bank engines assisted with shunting.

It is interesting to recall that when the first six of the S & D 2-8-0 locomotives were built in 1914 these were prohibited from using Bath M.P.D. and for many years some of these locomotives were shedded at Radstock. Also shedded here were the only locomotives to be built at Highbridge numbers 25A, 26A and 45A (known locally as the 'Dazzlers' (a full description is given in 'S & D Locomotive History' by D. Bradley and D. Milton (David & Charles)). These were employed on colliery shunting and were replaced in 1929 by two Sentinel 0-4-0 shunters, numbers 101 and 102.

As certain of the collieries could only be reached by way of a very low bridge (Tyning bridge but known locally as 'Marble Arch') of only 10' 10" height above rail level, the Sentinels were necessarily of restricted size. A picture of both the locomotives and 'Marble Arch' can be found in 'The Picture History of the Somerset and Dorset Railway' by Robin Atthill (David & Charles).

Connections were made with Ludlow's colliery east of the station (closed in 1950); this line also connected with the GWR goods yard and until 1966 was the only physical connection between the two systems. Just west of the station a siding left the up line and ran to Middle Pit (closed in 1933) and on to Clansdown (closed in 1929). After the closure of Middle Pit the line remained to serve Radstock gas works, which was adjacent, until its closure about 1950.

The North 'A' signal box of seventeen levers was closed on 23rd August, 1964 from which date the thirty two lever North 'B' was renamed Radstock North. At the same time the north crossover (outside 'A' Box) and goods shed siding were taken out of use.

Radstock An aerial view after closure of the S & D. Radstock North is in the foreground with Radstock South ex-GWR station in the centre of the picture. The new connection to the ex-GWR line just west of the North station put in on closure of the S & D can be seen. The GWR line itself had been cut short only about ¼ mile beyond the new connection. The line to Ludlow's colliery is in the foreground curving away left past the S & D loco shed. *Aerofilms*

Radstock   A view through the platforms with North 'B' box in background.
R.C. Riley

RADSTOCK

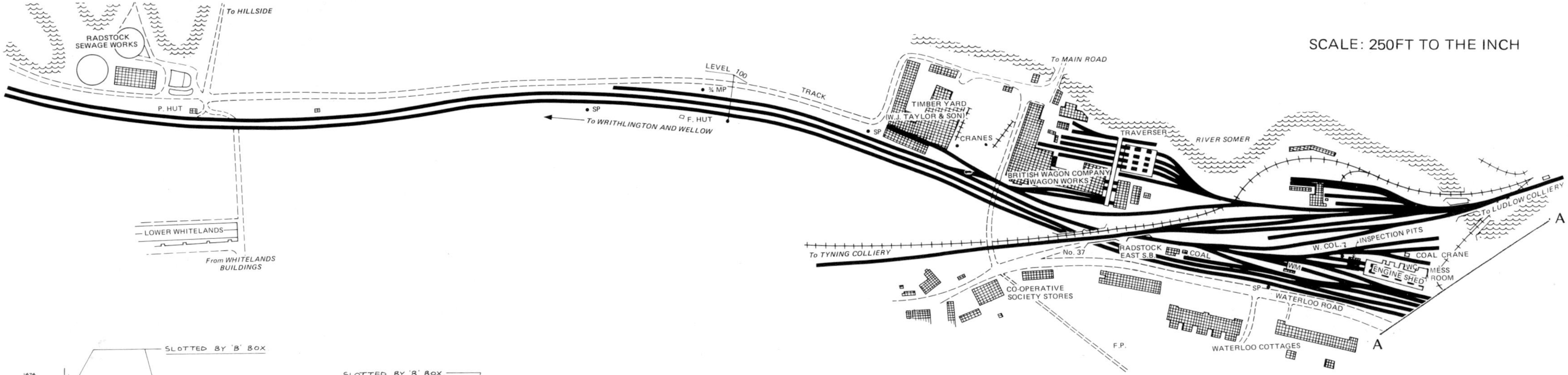

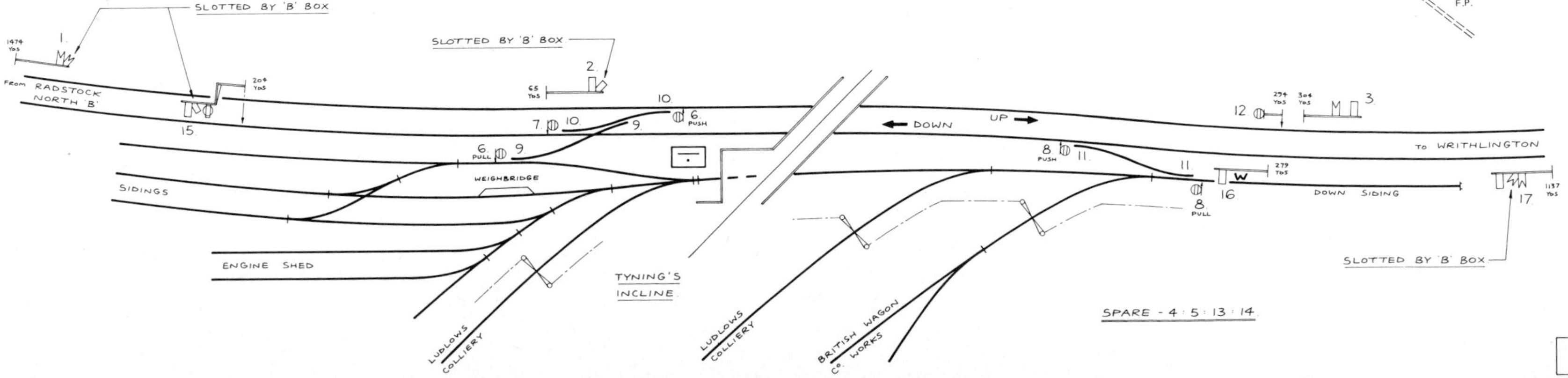

SCALE: 250FT TO THE INCH

To HILLSIDE

RADSTOCK
SEWAGE WORKS

LEVEL 100

TRACK

To MAIN ROAD

P. HUT

SP

¾ MP

F. HUT

SP

To WRITHLINGTON AND WELLOW

TIMBER YARD
W.J. TAYLOR & SON

CRANES

TRAVERSER

RIVER SOMER

To LUDLOW COLLIERY

LOWER WHITELANDS

From WHITELANDS
BUILDINGS

BRITISH WAGON COMPANY
WAGON WORKS

To TYNING COLLIERY

No. 37

RADSTOCK
EAST S.B.

COAL

W. COL. 2

INSPECTION PITS

A — A

WC
MESS
ROOM

COAL CRANE

WM

ENGINE SHED

CO-OPERATIVE
SOCIETY STORES

SP

WATERLOO ROAD

WATERLOO COTTAGES

F.P.

A — A

SLOTTED BY 'B' BOX

1474
Yds

1.

SLOTTED BY 'B' BOX

2

FROM RADSTOCK
NORTH 'B'

204
Yds

15

65
Yds

10

7   10

9

6
PUSH

12

25+   3o4
Yds   Yds

3

6
PULL

9

WEIGHBRIDGE

DOWN   UP

8
PUSH

11

11

279
Yds

W

To WRITHLINGTON

1137
Yds

SIDINGS

8
PULL

16

DOWN SIDING

W

17

ENGINE SHED

TYNING'S
INCLINE

SLOTTED BY 'B' BOX

LUDLOWS
COLLIERY

LUDLOWS
COLLIERY

BRITISH WAGON
Co. WORKS

SPARE - 4 : 5 : 13 : 14

RADSTOCK NORTH 'A'

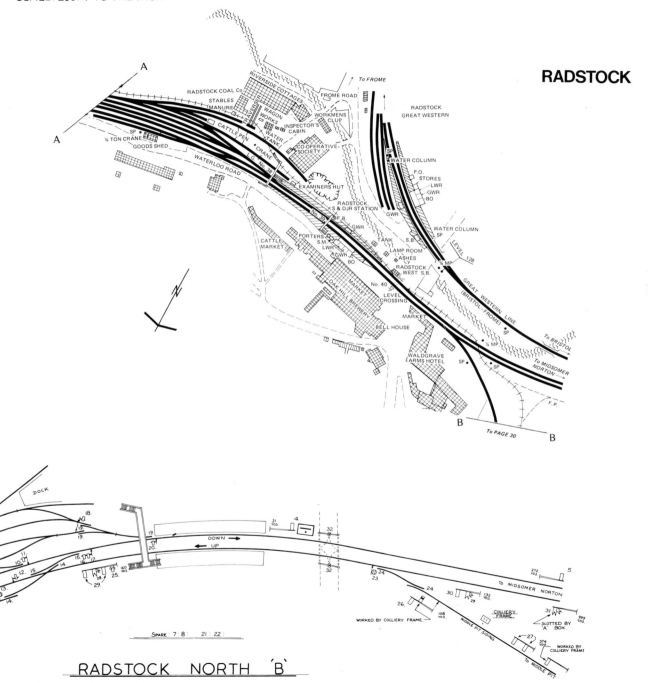

RADSTOCK

Radstock Radstock North 'B' box (1965).

M. O'Connor

RADSTOCK NORTH 'B'

Radstock The up platform looking east in 1951. *G.D. Pryer*

Radstock Looking west. *R.H. Clark*

Radstock An early view of the west end. *National Railway Museum, York*

Radstock The engine shed still in use in 1972; the diesel shunter was used on the coal trains. *M.J. Palmer*

Radstock   A good view of the station with North 'B' box in background; August 1964.
Bernard Robinson

Radstock   Radstock West signal box, later North 'B', looking towards Bath.
Lens of Sutton

RADSTOCK & AREA

Not the main S & D line

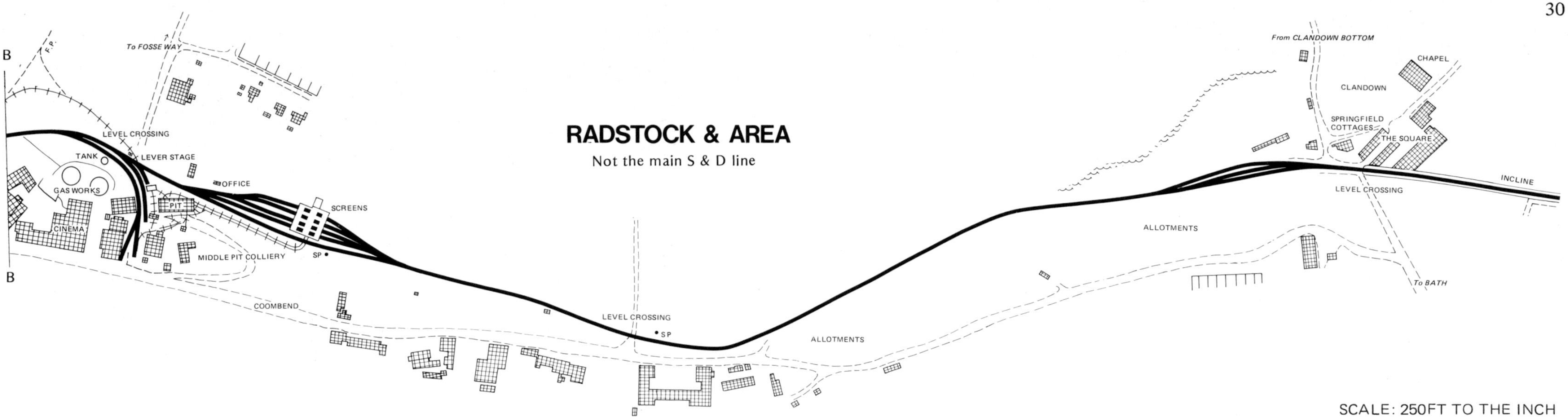

SCALE: 250FT TO THE INCH

NORTON HILL COLLIERY

SCALE: 250FT TO THE INCH

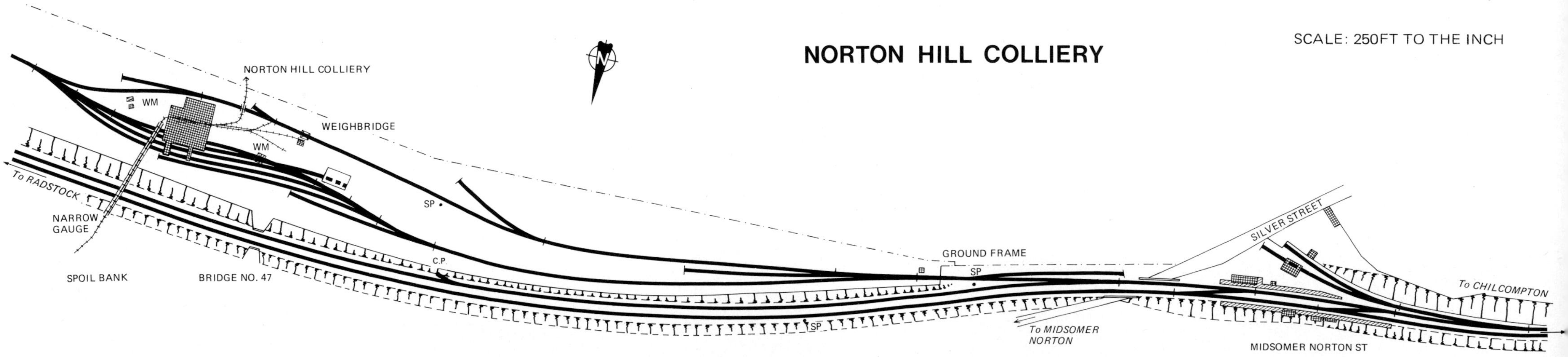

MIDSOMER NORTON

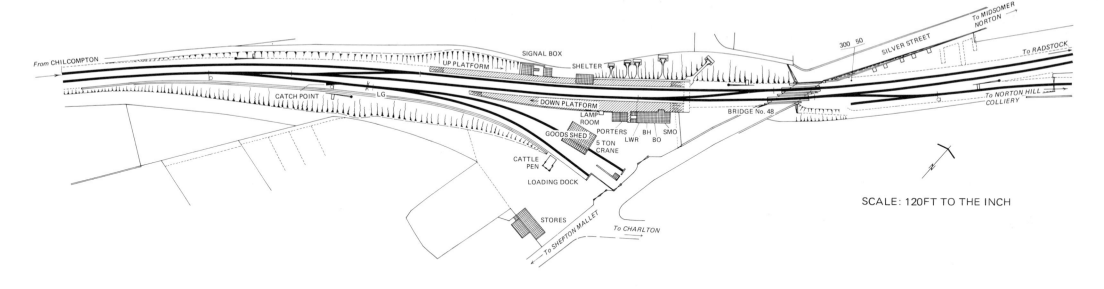

From CHILCOMPTON

SIGNAL BOX

UP PLATFORM

SHELTER

To MIDSOMER NORTON

SILVER STREET

To RADSTOCK

300 50

CATCH POINT

b

K

LG

DOWN PLATFORM

LAMP ROOM

GOODS SHED

PORTERS   BH   SMO

LWR   BO

5 TON CRANE

BRIDGE No. 48

To NORTON HILL COLLIERY

CATTLE PEN

LOADING DOCK

SCALE: 120FT TO THE INCH

STORES

To SHEPTON MALLET

To CHARLTON

Midsomer Norton   The station building.   *P.I. Clarke*

MIDSOMER NORTON

Opened: 20 June 1874
Closed: 7 March 1966 (to passengers)
                 15 June 1964 (to public goods traffic)
Renamings: 'Midsomer Norton' until 16 October 1898
                 'Midsomer Norton & Welton' until 26 September 1949
                 'Midsomer Norton Upper' (passenger station) thereafter
                 'Midsomer Norton South' (goods depot) from 25 September 1950
Plan date: 1921

Some two miles up the gradient from Radstock the small wayside station of Midsomer Norton was reached. As can be seen from the plan there were two short sidings one of which passed through a goods shed. Just before the station was reached from the Radstock direction a line trailed into the down main line which gave access to the sidings at Norton Hill Colliery (opened in 1900). The National Coal Board had their own steam locomotive which was employed on shunting the colliery yard.

A great pride was taken at Midsomer Norton in the appearance of the station. In particular the station gardens were a joy to behold and the station walked away with first prize in the 'Best Kept Station' competition for year after year. A most attractive sixteen lever signal box stood alongside the garden on the up platform; a block switch was provided to enable the box to switch out of circuit.

MIDSOMER NORTON

Midsomer Norton   The down platform.   *OPC collection*

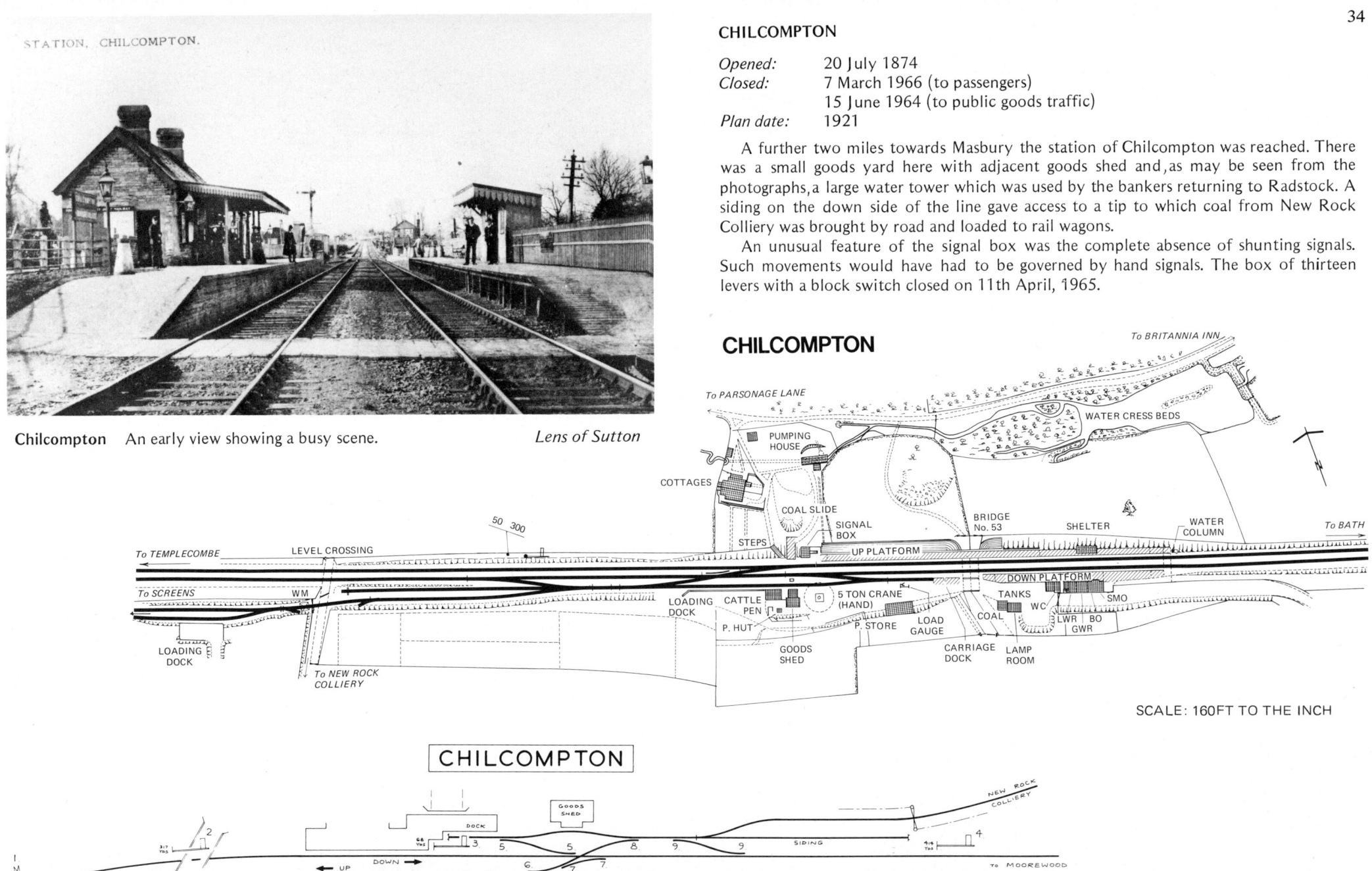

STATION, CHILCOMPTON.

Chilcompton   An early view showing a busy scene.

Lens of Sutton

CHILCOMPTON

Opened: 20 July 1874
Closed: 7 March 1966 (to passengers)
               15 June 1964 (to public goods traffic)
Plan date: 1921

A further two miles towards Masbury the station of Chilcompton was reached. There was a small goods yard here with adjacent goods shed and, as may be seen from the photographs, a large water tower which was used by the bankers returning to Radstock. A siding on the down side of the line gave access to a tip to which coal from New Rock Colliery was brought by road and loaded to rail wagons.

An unusual feature of the signal box was the complete absence of shunting signals. Such movements would have had to be governed by hand signals. The box of thirteen levers with a block switch closed on 11th April, 1965.

CHILCOMPTON

To BRITANNIA INN
To PARSONAGE LANE
WATER CRESS BEDS
PUMPING HOUSE
COTTAGES
COAL SLIDE
STEPS
SIGNAL BOX
BRIDGE No. 53
SHELTER
WATER COLUMN
To BATH
UP PLATFORM
To TEMPLECOMBE
LEVEL CROSSING
50 300
DOWN PLATFORM
To SCREENS
WM
LOADING DOCK
CATTLE PEN
5 TON CRANE (HAND)
TANKS
WC
SMO
P. HUT
P. STORE
LOAD GAUGE
COAL
LWR BO
GWR
LOADING DOCK
To NEW ROCK COLLIERY
GOODS SHED
CARRIAGE DOCK
LAMP ROOM

SCALE: 160FT TO THE INCH

CHILCOMPTON

To MIDSOMER NORTON SOUTH
GOODS SHED
DOCK
NEW ROCK COLLIERY
SIDING
To MOOREWOOD
UP   DOWN

Chilcompton The neat station building on the down platform. *OPC collection*

Chilcompton The goods yard and the connection to New Rock Colliery can be seen here. *OPC collection*

Chilcompton The attractive and well preserved signal box (1960). *R.C. Riley*

Chilcompton Looking towards Midsomer Norton. *OPC Collection*

Moorewood Sidings   The compact 19 lever signal box.
                                                    R. Atthill

MOOREWOOD SIDINGS

Plan date: 1921

Originally the sidings on the up side of the layout (opened in 1901) which gave access to the Emborough Quarries had been controlled by a ground frame known as 'Old Down' siding. However in 1914 a signal box, the last to be provided on the line, was opened at this location. Later stone crushing plants were built here and coal from Moorewood Colliery was loaded into rail wagons. By 1930 both these operations had ceased and the signal box was reduced to a one shift basis purely for the Emborough stone traffic. The down sidings were used for storing wagons and the nineteen lever signal box finally closed on 21st June, 1965.

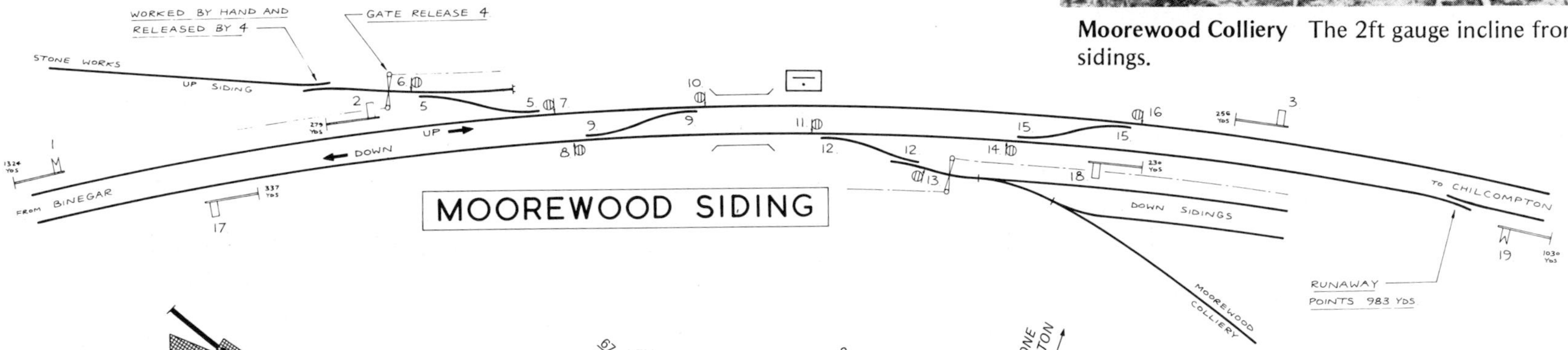

Moorewood Colliery   The 2ft gauge incline from the colliery to the sidings.
                                                    British Rail

WORKED BY HAND AND RELEASED BY 4
GATE RELEASE 4
STONE WORKS
UP SIDING
FROM BINEGAR
DOWN   UP
TO CHILCOMPTON
DOWN SIDINGS
MOOREWOOD COLLIERY
RUNAWAY POINTS 983 YDS

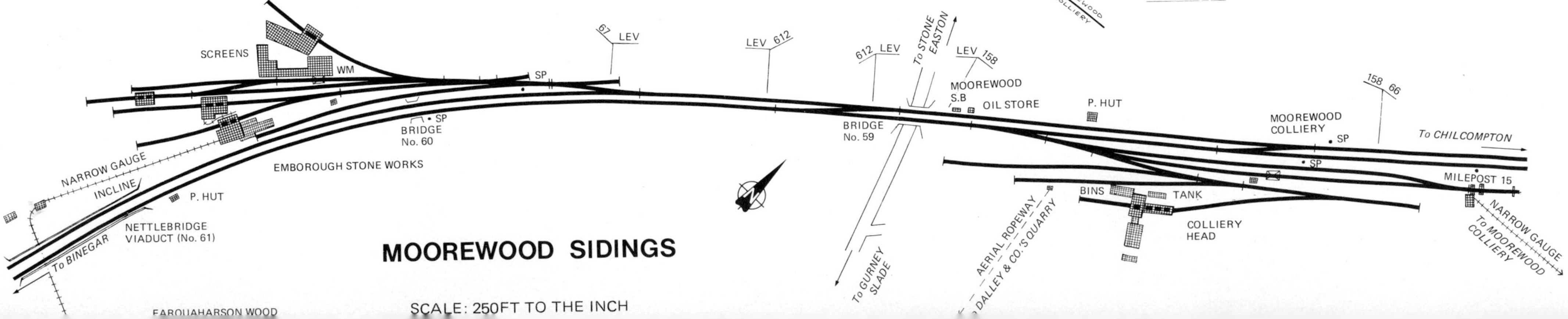

MOOREWOOD SIDING

SCREENS
WM
67 LEV
LEV 612
612 LEV
To STONE EASTON
LEV 158
MOOREWOOD S.B
OIL STORE
P. HUT
158 66
MOOREWOOD COLLIERY
To CHILCOMPTON
NARROW GAUGE INCLINE
P. HUT
BRIDGE No. 60
EMBOROUGH STONE WORKS
BRIDGE No. 59
MILEPOST 15
NETTLEBRIDGE VIADUCT (No. 61)
To BINEGAR
To GURNEY SLADE
AERIAL ROPEWAY DALLEY & CO'S QUARRY
BINS
TANK
COLLIERY HEAD
NARROW GAUGE To MOOREWOOD COLLIERY

MOOREWOOD SIDINGS

FARQUAHARSON WOOD

SCALE: 250FT TO THE INCH

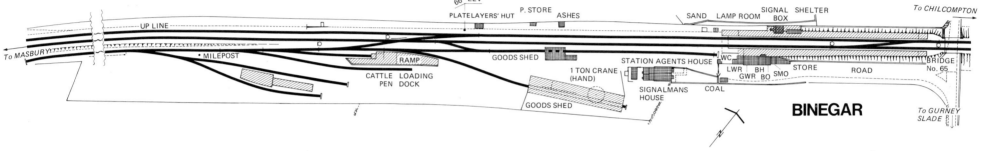

MENDIPS STONE WORKS

To BINEGAR

To BINEGAR
178 LEV
SP

To CHILCOMPTON
SP

½ MP
SP
BRIDGE
No. 65
W.B.

MENDIPS
STONE
WORKS

To GURNEY
SLADE

QUARRY RLY

SCALE: 160FT TO THE INCH

66 LEV
PLATELAYERS' HUT
P. STORE
ASHES

SAND LAMP ROOM
SIGNAL
BOX
SHELTER

To CHILCOMPTON

UP LINE

To MASBURY

MILEPOST

RAMP

CATTLE LOADING
PEN DOCK

GOODS SHED

1 TON CRANE
(HAND)

STATION AGENTS HOUSE

WC
LWR BH
GWR BO SMO
STORE
ROAD

BRIDGE
No. 65

SIGNALMANS
HOUSE

COAL

GOODS SHED

BINEGAR

To GURNEY
SLADE

Binegar Towards Chilcompton.

G. Judd

BINEGAR

Opened: 20 July 1874
Closed: 7 March 1966 (to passengers)
              10 June 1963 (to goods)
Plan date: 1921

    Approaching Binegar from Moorewood a siding from the Mendips Stone Works trailed into the down line. The sidings were fed by an aerial ropeway from the quarries. There was a substantial stone building near the down platform. This had originally been owned by the Oakhill Brewery and was the terminus of a two mile long light railway of 3 feet gauge which carried the Oakhill Brewery's stout. Two 0-4-0 tank locomotives, *Oakhill* and *Mendip* worked this line, opened in 1904 and closed in 1921. It was after closure that the large stone built building was converted to a standard gauge goods shed. On the up platform stood a sturdy signal box and adjacent shelter. Beyond the platforms on the down side were several other sidings including two serving cattle pens.

    Down freight trains which were banked as far as Masbury summit picked up a 'Banking key' at Binegar. This permitted the Bank engine, having seen the brake van pass over the summit at Masbury, to return 'wrong line' to Binegar. A special key lever, number five in the signal box, controlled the release of the key and provided the necessary security of interlocking to enable the wrong direction movement to be made safely.

Binegar   The down platform building and canopy with signal box opposite.   *R.C. Riley*

Binegar   The special Whitaker's apparatus from which the banking engine key was obtained.   *R. Atthill*

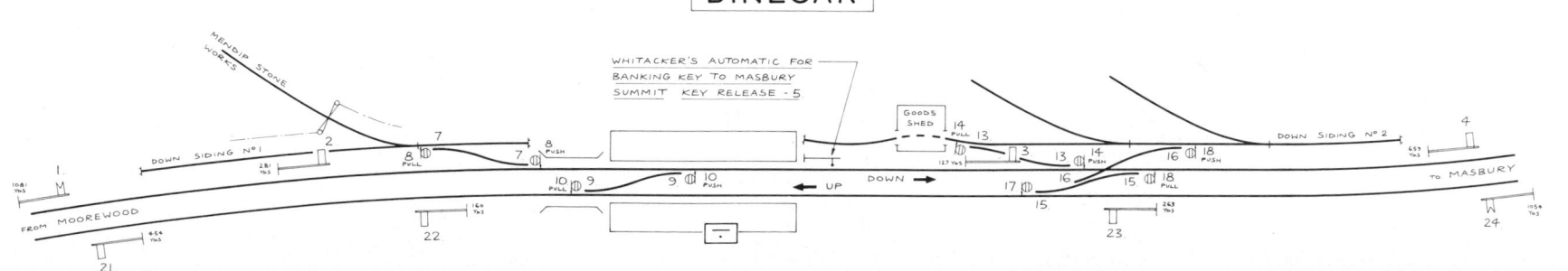

BINEGAR

Binegar   Two banking engines stand outside the signal box in July 1957.
Photomatic

Binegar   A double headed express approaches the up platform.
OPC collection

MASBURY

Opened: 20 July 1874
Closed: 7 March 1966 (to passengers)
              10 June 1963 (to goods)
              The passenger station was unstaffed from 26 September 1938
Plan date: 1921

As may be seen from the photograph the up platform at Masbury was quite full of buildings whilst the down platform merely contained a simple shelter. Starting from the north end of the up platform one came across a substantial stone building containing the booking office and waiting room. Next came the signal box which contained twenty levers and had a block switch and then, alongside, the substantial station master's house, again built of stone. The ground floor of this building was surmounted by a stone carving of an imaginary mediaeval castle and the Gothic legend *Maesbury Castle*; this carving can clearly be seen in the various photographs.

A small goods yard was provided on the up side of the line whilst the sidings on the down side were extended in the Second World War to serve a US Army Camp. These were all lifted in 1959 whilst the up siding was taken out of use when the signal box was closed on 1st July, 1964.

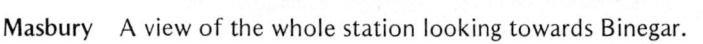

Masbury   A view of the whole station looking towards Binegar.   *R.C. Riley*

MASBURY

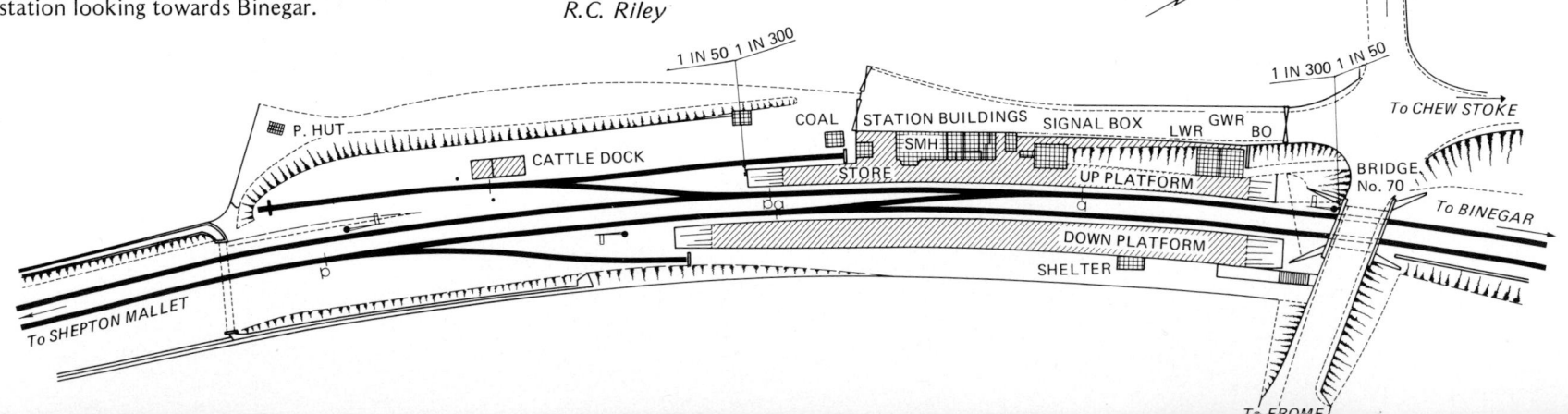

SCALE: 100FT TO THE INCH

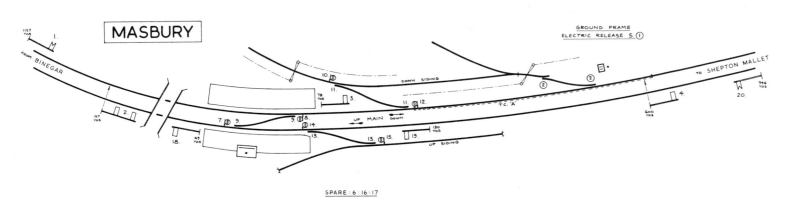

MASBURY

Masbury A view of the signal box in September 1965 (it closed July 1964).
M. O'Connor

Masbury The carving above the bay window of the station house can be seen (September 1965).
M. O'Connor

Masbury Looking towards Shepton Mallet.
Lens of Sutton

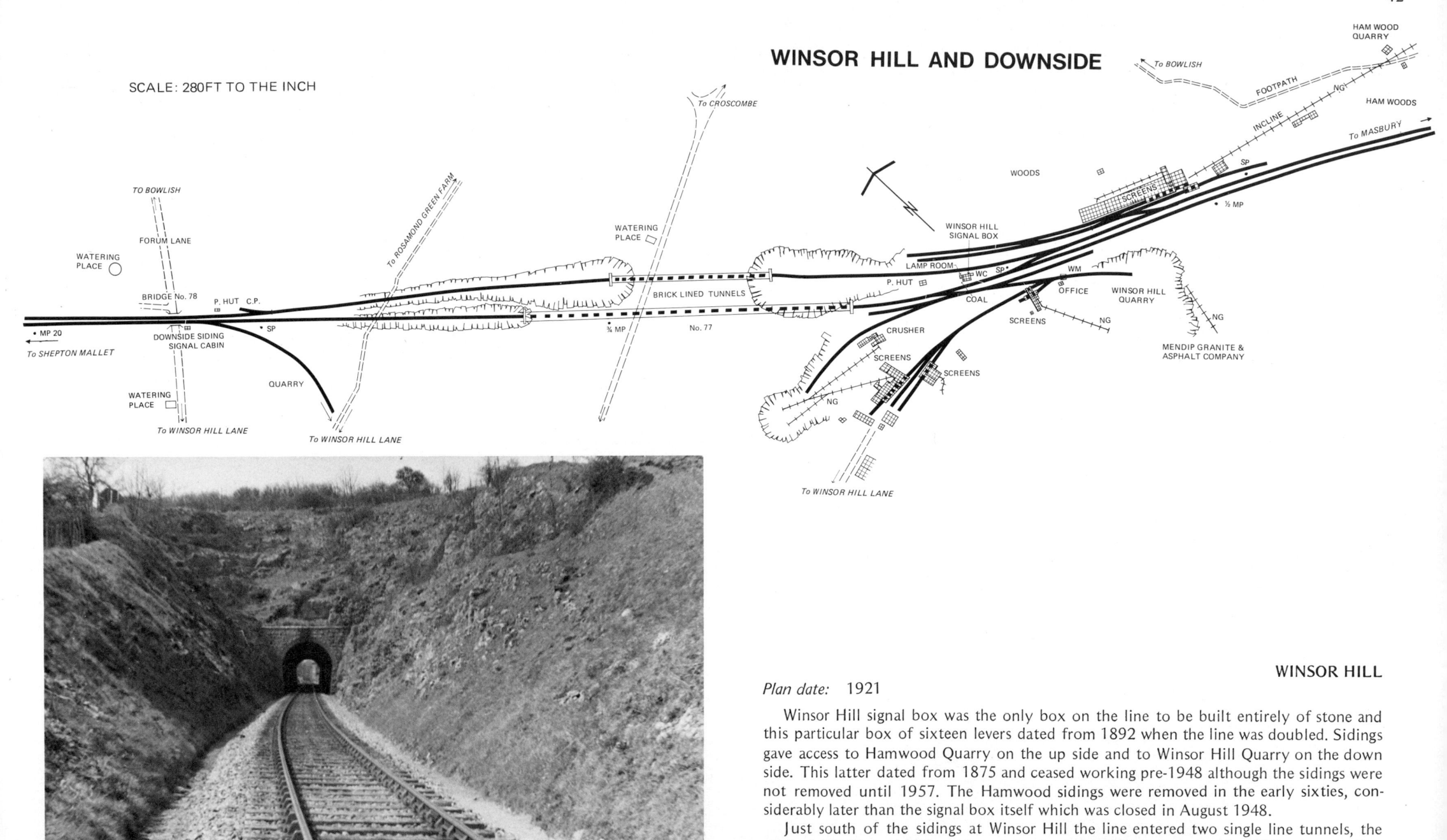

WINSOR HILL AND DOWNSIDE

SCALE: 280FT TO THE INCH

To Bowlish

To Croscombe

HAM WOOD QUARRY

FOOTPATH

NG

HAM WOODS

INCLINE

To MASBURY

WOODS

SP

½ MP

WINSOR HILL SIGNAL BOX

LAMP ROOM

WC SP

WM

P. HUT

OFFICE

COAL

WINSOR HILL QUARRY

SCREENS

NG

NG

TO BOWLISH

FORUM LANE

WATERING PLACE

To ROSAMOND GREEN FARM

WATERING PLACE

CRUSHER

MENDIP GRANITE & ASPHALT COMPANY

WATERING PLACE

BRIDGE No. 78

P. HUT C.P.

BRICK LINED TUNNELS

SCREENS

SCREENS

MP 20

SP

¾ MP

No. 77

To SHEPTON MALLET

DOWNSIDE SIDING SIGNAL CABIN

NG

QUARRY

WATERING PLACE

To WINSOR HILL LANE

To WINSOR HILL LANE

To WINSOR HILL LANE

WINSOR HILL

Plan date: 1921

Winsor Hill signal box was the only box on the line to be built entirely of stone and this particular box of sixteen levers dated from 1892 when the line was doubled. Sidings gave access to Hamwood Quarry on the up side and to Winsor Hill Quarry on the down side. This latter dated from 1875 and ceased working pre-1948 although the sidings were not removed until 1957. The Hamwood sidings were removed in the early sixties, considerably later than the signal box itself which was closed in August 1948.

Just south of the sidings at Winsor Hill the line entered two single line tunnels, the original Old Tunnel 239 yards and the later New Tunnel, opened in 1892, when the line was doubled, 126 yards.

Winsor Hill Approach to south portal of New Tunnel.

R.H. Clark

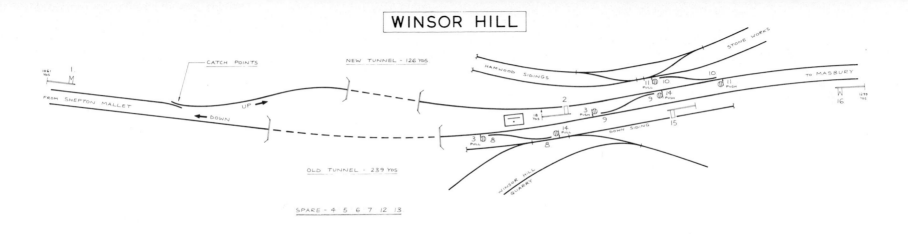

SPARE - 4 5 6 7 12 13

DOWNSIDE QUARRY SIDING

Plan date: 1921

Between Winsor Hill and Shepton Mallet and situated on the down line was Downside siding operated by a ground frame by means of a key electrically released from Winsor Hill signal box. This siding closed in 1940.

Winsor Hill Signal Box   Close-up view; derelict . (July 1953.)   *R.H. Clark*

Winsor Hill Tunnels   View looking at the New Tunnel (left) and the Old Tunnel (right).
R.H. Clark

Shepton Mallet   Looking north.   *Lens of Sutton*

SHEPTON MALLET (CHARLTON ROAD)

Opened:	20 July 1874
Closed:	7 March 1966 (to passengers)
	10 June 1963 (to goods)
Renamings:	'Shepton Mallet' (passenger station) until October 1883
	'Shepton Mallet' (goods depot) until 26 September 1949
	then 'Shepton Mallet (Charlton Road)' to closure
Plan date:	1921

Approaching Shepton Mallet from the north a train first crossed the Bath Road viaduct (118 yards) — this structure collapsed during a gale in February 1946 and was not rebuilt until August of that year, single line working being operated in the interval controlled from the temporary Waterloo Road signal box. Next the Charlton viaduct (317 yards) was crossed before the extensive layout at Shepton Mallet was reached.

The main buildings at Shepton Mallet were on the up platform. On the down side stood the twenty six lever signal box and a small waiting room; just beyond the southern end of the down platform stood a water crane at which most down freight trains called to take water.

The down yard contained sidings serving a stone crushing plant and the signal inspector for the whole line had his office here together with the department's workshops (until 1930). The up yard contained the general traffic sidings, commodiously laid out, together with a medium sized goods shed and 5 ton yard crane. All the sidings were out of use by 1964.

Immediately south of the station layout the Somerset & Dorset passed under the East Somerset line of the GWR which connected Yatton, on the Bristol–Taunton main line, to Witham on the Westbury–Taunton section of the GWR's trunk route to Devon and Cornwall.

Shepton Mallet   Down sidings at right, looking towards Winsor Hill.   *OPC collection*

Shepton Mallet   Looking north towards Winsor Hill.   *OPC collection*

SHEPTON MALLET

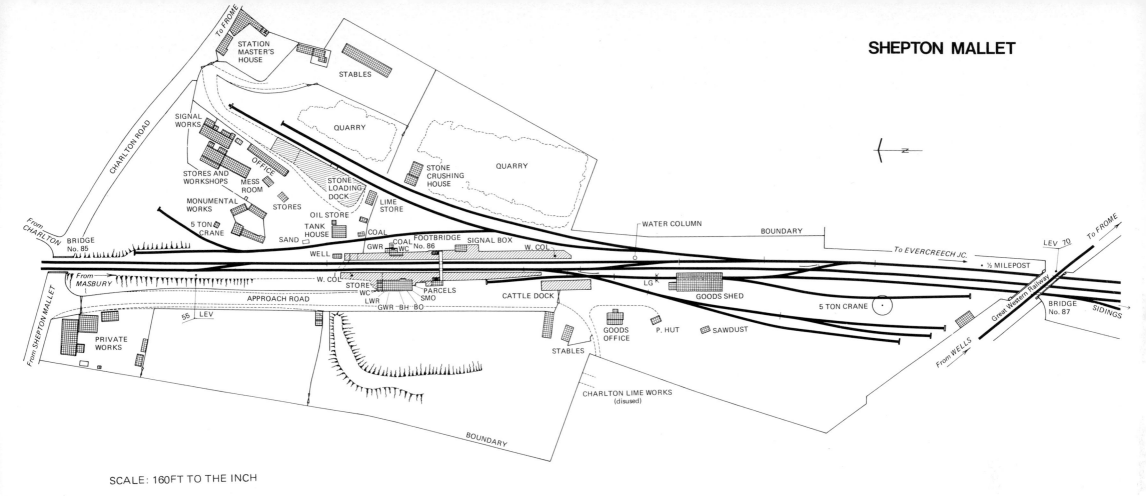

SCALE: 160FT TO THE INCH

SHEPTON MALLET

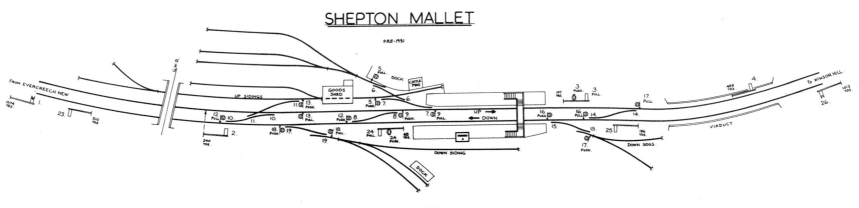

Shepton Mallet   Looking south towards the cattle dock and goods shed.   OPC Collection

Shepton Mallet   The down side shelter and water tank.   OPC Collection

Shepton Mallet   A general view looking towards Evercreech.   OPC Collection

Shepton Mallet   Looking north towards Charlton viaduct.   R.C. Riley

EVERCREECH NEW STATION

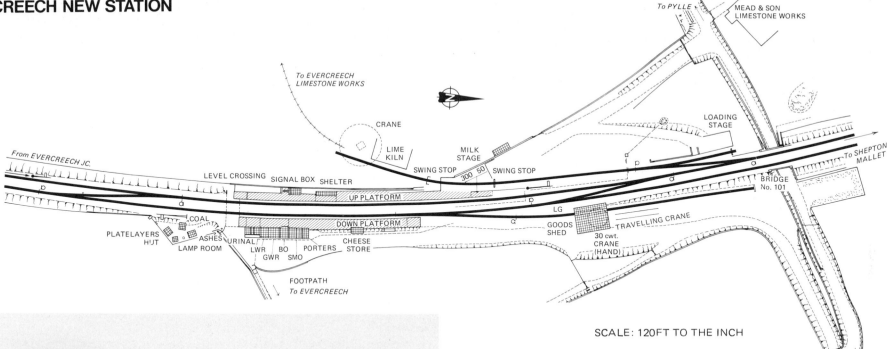

To EVERCREECH
LIMESTONE WORKS

To PYLLE

MEAD & SON
LIMESTONE WORKS

CRANE

LIME
KILN

MILK
STAGE

LOADING
STAGE

From EVERCREECH JC.

SWING STOP   300 50   SWING STOP

To SHEPTON
MALLET

LEVEL CROSSING   SIGNAL BOX   SHELTER

UP PLATFORM

BRIDGE
No. 101

DOWN PLATFORM

LG

PLATELAYERS
HUT

ASHES   URINAL

COAL

GOODS
SHED

30 cwt.
CRANE
(HAND)

TRAVELLING CRANE

LAMP ROOM   LWR   BO   PORTERS   CHEESE
GWR   SMO   STORE

FOOTPATH
To EVERCREECH

To EVERCREECH

SCALE: 120FT TO THE INCH

Evercreech New   A general view looking north.

R.C. Riley

EVERCREECH NEW

Opened: 20 July 1874
Closed: 7 March 1966 (to passengers)
                1 July 1964 (to goods)
Plan date: 1921

Evercreech New, well sited on the edge of its large village, was quite a small station. The main station buildings were at the southern end of the down platform whilst the tall attractive signal box (of twenty levers and provided with a block switch) stood opposite on the up platform. This was the second box at this station, the first having been burnt down in October 1918 and not rebuilt until January 1920, although a temporary ground frame was installed for the intervening period.

A medium sized goods shed, built in stone, stood on the down side whilst the small up yard dealt at one time with considerable milk traffic as well as lime from the Evercreech Lime and Stone Co. All the sidings together with the signal box were closed on 11th October, 1964.

Evercreech New   The goods yard and goods shed looking north.   *OPC collection*

Evercreech New   Looking south.   *Lens of Sutton*

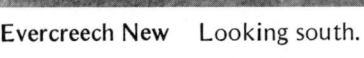

Evercreech New   A close up of the compact signal box.   *OPC collection*

Evercreech New   The station building.   *OPC collection*

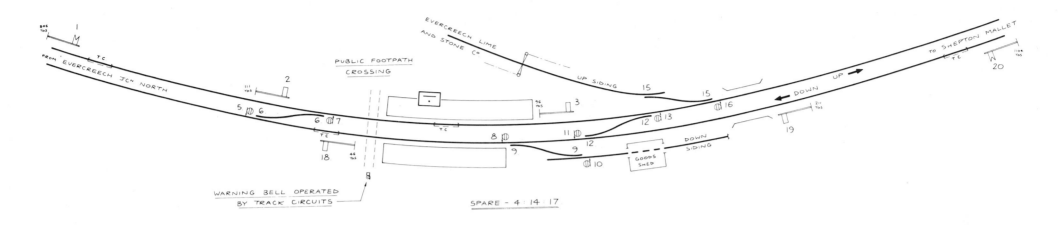

EVERCREECH NEW

PUBLIC FOOTPATH
CROSSING

EVERCREECH LIME
AND STONE CO

TO SHEPTON MALLET

FROM EVERCREECH JCN NORTH

UP SIDING

DOWN SIDING

GOODS SHED

WARNING BELL OPERATED
BY TRACK CIRCUITS

SPARE - 4 : 14 : 17

Evercreech New   In one photograph the whole of the facilities available can be seen.   *D. Milton*

Evercreech New   The south end of the platform showing foot crossing.   *OPC collection*

Evercreech Junction   The station master's house, level crossing and water tank, seen here in 1965.

OPC Collection

50

Evercreech Jc. S & D No. 12 at Evercreech Jc. This class of locomotive worked the Bath—Bournemouth expresses until 1891. *R. Atthill*

EVERCREECH JUNCTION

Opened: 3 February 1862
Closed: 7 March 1966 (to passengers)
               29 November 1965 (to goods)
Renaming: 'Evercreech' until 20 July 1874 when the line to Bath junction was opened and Evercreech New was brought into use.
Plan date: c. 1930s.

Trains from Bath entering Evercreech Junction had to slow to 25 mph as they traversed a sharp left hand curve, whilst those on the single line branch from Highbridge had a straight "run in", reflecting the original main line status of this branch. After passing the thirty two lever North signal box, the principal marshalling yard at the Junction, consisting of six roads, was seen on the up side of the line and then the well laid out station and goods yard was reached.

The down platform contained attractive stone built station buildings and the large station master's house. A footbridge just past the latter connected the two platforms and at the southern end of the up platform behind the footbridge stood the tall South box which contained twenty six levers which controlled a level crossing and access to the goods yard.

On the down side of the line just north of the station was the small goods yard. This contained cattle pens, small goods shed and two cranes, one of seven ton capacity and a smaller one ton crane. A third yard existed at Evercreech Jc.; this was the New yard consisting of five sidings and was on the down side of the single line from Burnham. Shunting in the various yards was continuous through the day and night.

Evercreech Jc. Looking south through the station, showing rail entrance to goods yard. *R.H. Clark*

Evercreech Jc. The attractive buildings on the down platform. *R.C. Riley*

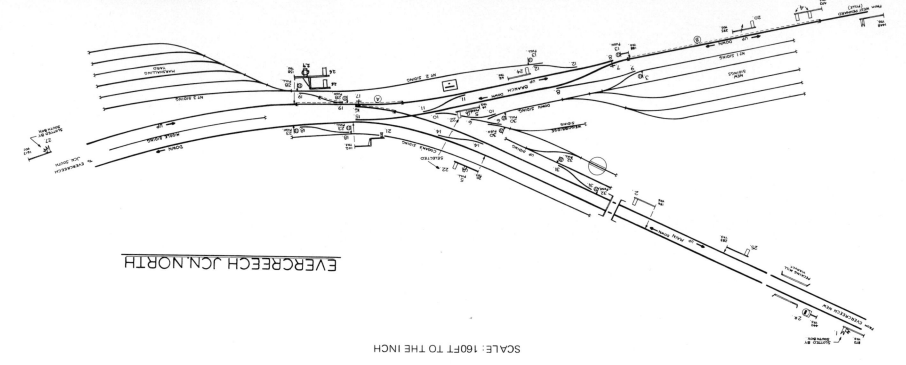

EVERCREECH JCN. NORTH

SCALE: 160FT TO THE INCH

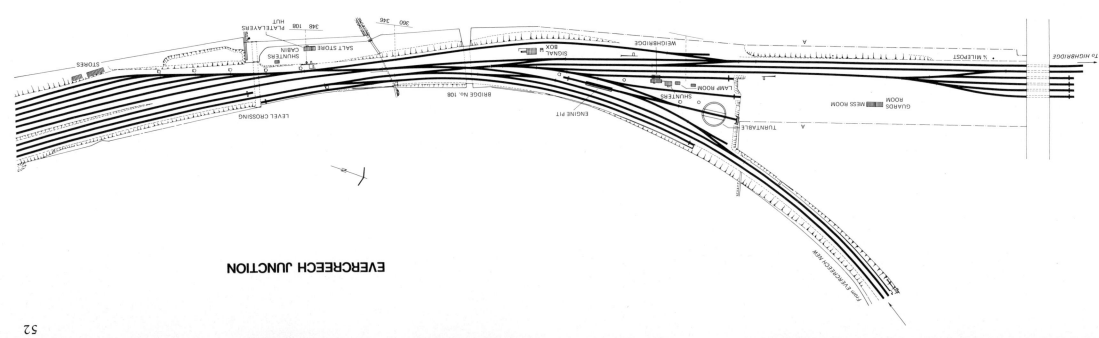

EVERCREECH JUNCTION

EVERCREECH JC. SOUTH

1581 YDS.

3

SLOTTED BY NORTH BOX.

from EVERCREECH JCN. NORTH

2156 YDS.

309 YDS.

SIDING

DOWN

UP

318 YDS.

4.

17 Pull

8

8 Pull

15 Pull.Y

17 Pull

13 Pull.Y

14 Pull

16 Pull

15 Push

13 Push

14 Push

16 Push

17 Push

20

231 YDS.

10

10

12

14 Pull

RBC.

A

B

11

SIDINGS.

5

809 YDS.

5

25

25.

25

26

26

26

18 Pull

18 Push

19

19

21

116 YDS.

(200 YDS.)

523 YDS.

6

To COLE

22

809 YDS.

SLOTTED BY NORTH BOX

Y = YELLOW ARM

SPARE : 1 : 2 : 7 : 9 : 23 : 24

To COLE

WATER COLUMN

STATION MASTER'S HOUSE

LEVEL CROSSING

TANK

SHED

GOODS SHED

STATION BUILDINGS

1 TON RADIAL CRANE

LOADING GAUGE

7 TON CRANE (HAND)

CATTLE PEN

DOWN

UP PLATFORM

DAIRY

STORE

WATER COLUMN

STATION BUILDINGS

SIGNAL BOX

RAILWAY HOTEL

GENTS

EVERCREECH JUNCTION

CATTLE PEN

BRIDGE No. 109

LAMP ROOM

WATER COLUMN

SLAUGHTER HOUSE

LEVEL CROSSING

UP

DOWN

SALT STORE

SHOWERS

PLATELAYERS HUT

TELEGRAPH DEPT. STORES

SCALE: 160FT TO THE INCH

Evercreech Jc.   A special buffer stop with three link coupling at the north end of the middle siding which continued into the station (shown on plan above just short of the level crossing). This was to prevent vehicles standing in the siding running down the 1 in 100 gradient into the station.

M.J. Palmer

53

Evercreech Jc.   The up platform buildings.   *OPC collection*

Evercreech Jc.   View from the footbridge looking north; July 1953.   *R.H. Clark*

Evercreech Jc.   Collett 0-6-0 ex G.W.R. No. 3206 at the station with a Highbridge-Templecombe train in 1962.   *Bernard Robinson*

Evercreech Jc.   The main station building on the down platform.   *M.J. Palmer*

COLE

Opened: 3 February 1862
Closed: 7 March 1966 (to passengers)
5 April 1965 (to goods)
Plan date: 1921

Cole was the most northerly station of the former Dorset Central railway which in 1862 joined with the Somerset Central Railway (from Burnham to north of Cole) to form the Somerset and Dorset Railway. The main building was on the down platform and was stone built. Of typical Dorset Central design it had high gables and tall chimneys and had no canopy. On the up platform, opposite, was a small wooden shelter and as will be discerned from the photographs this stood on an extension at a slightly higher level of the former short up platform.

The small fourteen lever wooden signal box (provided with a block switch) was at the southern end of the up platform; this was built in LSWR style and apart from breaking the section from Evercreech Jc. South to Wincanton, controlled access to the small goods yard on the down side. The yard closed on 5th April, 1965 and the signal box finally closed on 31st May, 1965.

Cole Collett 0-6-0 No. 2204 heads a southbound goods through Cole; August 1962.

Bernard Robinson

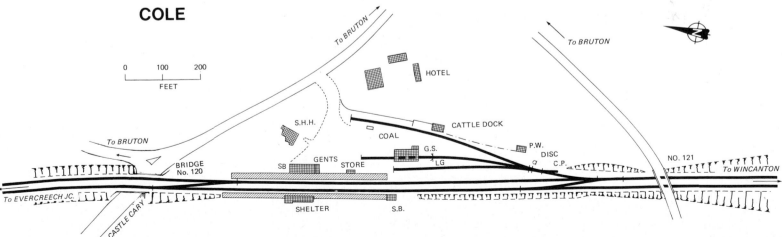

COLE

55

Cole General view of the station and yard looking north, July 1953. *R.H. Clark*

Cole The small signal box. *R. Atthill*

Cole Class 2P No. 40563 heads south in July 1959. *R.C. Riley*

Cole Towards Wincanton. *Lens of Sutton*

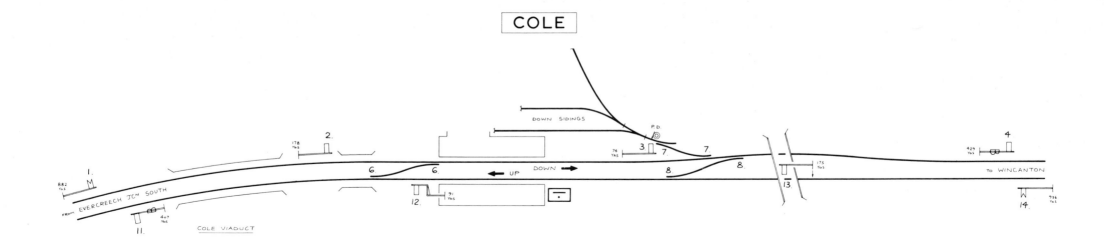

COLE

DOWN SIDINGS

P.D.

178 Yds

2.

74 Yds

3

7

7

4

429 Yds

4

882 Yds

1.

From EVERCREECH JCN SOUTH

6

6

← UP

DOWN →

8

8

175 Yds

To WINCANTON

91 Yds

12

13

14

736 Yds

407 Yds

11.

COLE VIADUCT

SPARE – 5 PULL : 5 PUSH : 9 PULL : 9 PUSH : 10 PULL : 10 PUSH.

Cole   Ex-LMS 4F No. 44422 arrives with a southbound train on 18th July, 1959.

R.C. Riley

Cole   Towards Evercreech.

OPC Collection

Wincanton

A charming early view looking towards Cole.

G. Judd collection

WINCANTON

Opened: November 1861
Closed: 7 March 1966 (to passengers)
                5 April 1965 (to public goods traffic)
Plan date: 1921

The fourteen lever elevated signal box which had a block switch, controlled a fairly large layout although a compact one. In the goods yard there was a loading dock which at one time saw a great deal of horse box traffic in connection with Wincanton Races. In addition cattle pens and a carriage loading dock were provided. The small goods shed housed a 30 cwt hand crane whilst a large 7 ton hand crane was available in the yard. In 1933 the Cow and Gate sidings shown on the signalling plan were installed and the station

dealt with a large number of milk tanks forwarded by rail to the London area.

The station retained most (but not all) of its lower quadrant signals (with wooden arms) to time of closure. It was one of the first stations on the system to be illuminated by gas, the fittings for which were ordered by the Dorset Central Company shortly before amalgamation with the Somerset Central in 1862.

Points No. 9 (the crossover at the south end of the station) were taken out of use in October 1964. The goods shed road was extended southward, and the trailing lead into the down main line moved likewise, presumably, at the time of putting in the Cow & Gate sidings in 1933, but the exact date is not known.

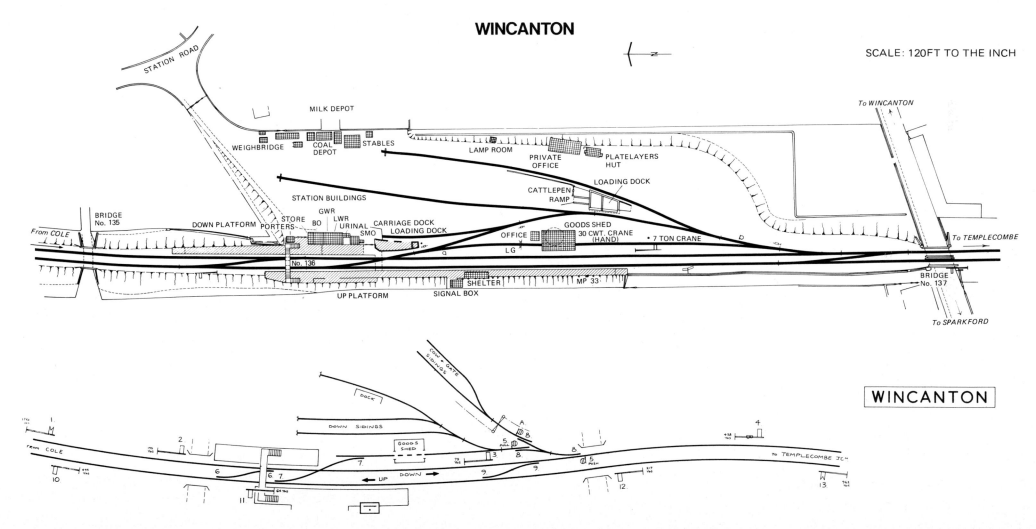

SCALE: 120FT TO THE INCH

Wincanton   An 1883 photograph looking towards Templecombe; a Johnson 0-6-0 stands on an up goods.

R. Atthill

Wincanton   Looking south towards Templecombe.   *Lens of Sutton*

Wincanton   Looking south, showing crossover to goods yard on left.   *Lens of Sutton*

Wincanton   The elevated signal box and staggered platforms will be noted.   *R.C. Riley*

Lower:	*Opened:*	1862
	Closed:	17 January 1887
Lower Platform:	*Opened:*	17 January 1887
	Closed:	3 January 1966
Lower (Goods)		
Yard:	*Closed:*	5 May 1950

(LSWR): The top station was opened by the Salisbury & Yeovil Railway on 7 May 1860 S & D trains commenced to use the bay platforms in March 1870

Plan date: 1921

Approaching Templecombe from the north trains passed over Horsington level crossing, until 1933 the site of Templecombe No. 3 Junction box. Just south of the level crossing was the junction, the left hand single line (which quickly became double) leading to the goods yard and engine shed; until closure of No. 3 Junction the left hand line had been double throughout. The right hand double line led to the former Templecombe No. 2 Junction (renamed simply Templecombe Junction in 1933 when it took over control of the former No. 3 Junction).

The goods yard at Templecombe was a scene of considerable activity inasmuch as all up freight trains worked here, together with down freight trains (except those which ran direct to Templecombe LSWR station via Templecombe Junction). Transfer trips were worked to and from the upper yard located west of the LSWR station, together with many light engine movements to and from the shed, in connection with the complex engine workings pulling and pushing through Somerset and Dorset trains to and from the LSWR station via Templecombe Junction. A full description of these engine movements can be found in Ivo Peters' 'The Somerset and Dorset Railway' published by OPC.

Between the engine shed (and its associated sidings) and the single line leading to Broadstone lay the site of the original Dorset Central station at Templecombe which closed in 1887. Also here was the old Templecombe No. 1 Junction signal box which gave access to the single line to Broadstone at the southern end of the layout; the connection lay just north of the overbridge carrying the LSWR from Waterloo to Exeter. This box and the connection were taken out of use on 16th January, 1887.

Most trains took the right hand line at No. 3 Junction and at Templecombe No. 2 Junction (later Templecombe Junction) the double line again divided, the left hand being single and continuing to Broadstone. The right hand double line at the junction continued on into the LSWR station at which nearly all Somerset and Dorset trains called; the exceptions were some of the through summer Saturday trains. Until 1933 there was a small 13 lever S & D signal box, Templecombe 'B', almost at the platform end which controlled movements from Templecombe No. 2 Junction but in that year it was closed and the signalling was taken over by the main Templecombe 'A' box.

S & D trains used the northern face of the up main line island platform at the LSWR station and S & D freight trains ran through this platform to gain access to the upper yard.

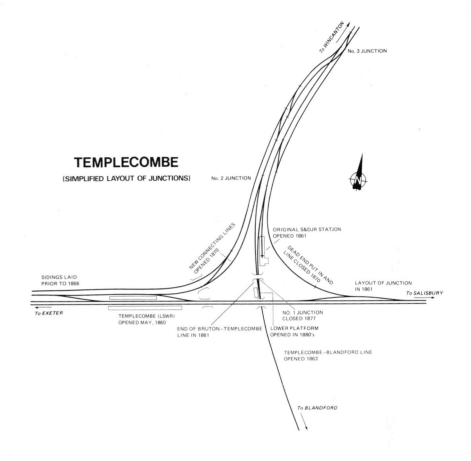

TEMPLECOMBE

(SIMPLIFIED LAYOUT OF JUNCTIONS)

Templecombe Junction was a forty four lever box of wooden construction and the largest signal box on the line. Just five chains beyond the box and the junction, on the single line to Broadstone, stood Templecombe Lower Platform; this was built on the up side of the single line in 1887, when the former Dorset Central station in what later became the engine yard was closed. Few trains called here, although, because of its close proximity to the shed, some trains which did not call at the upper LSWR station stopped here for crew change.

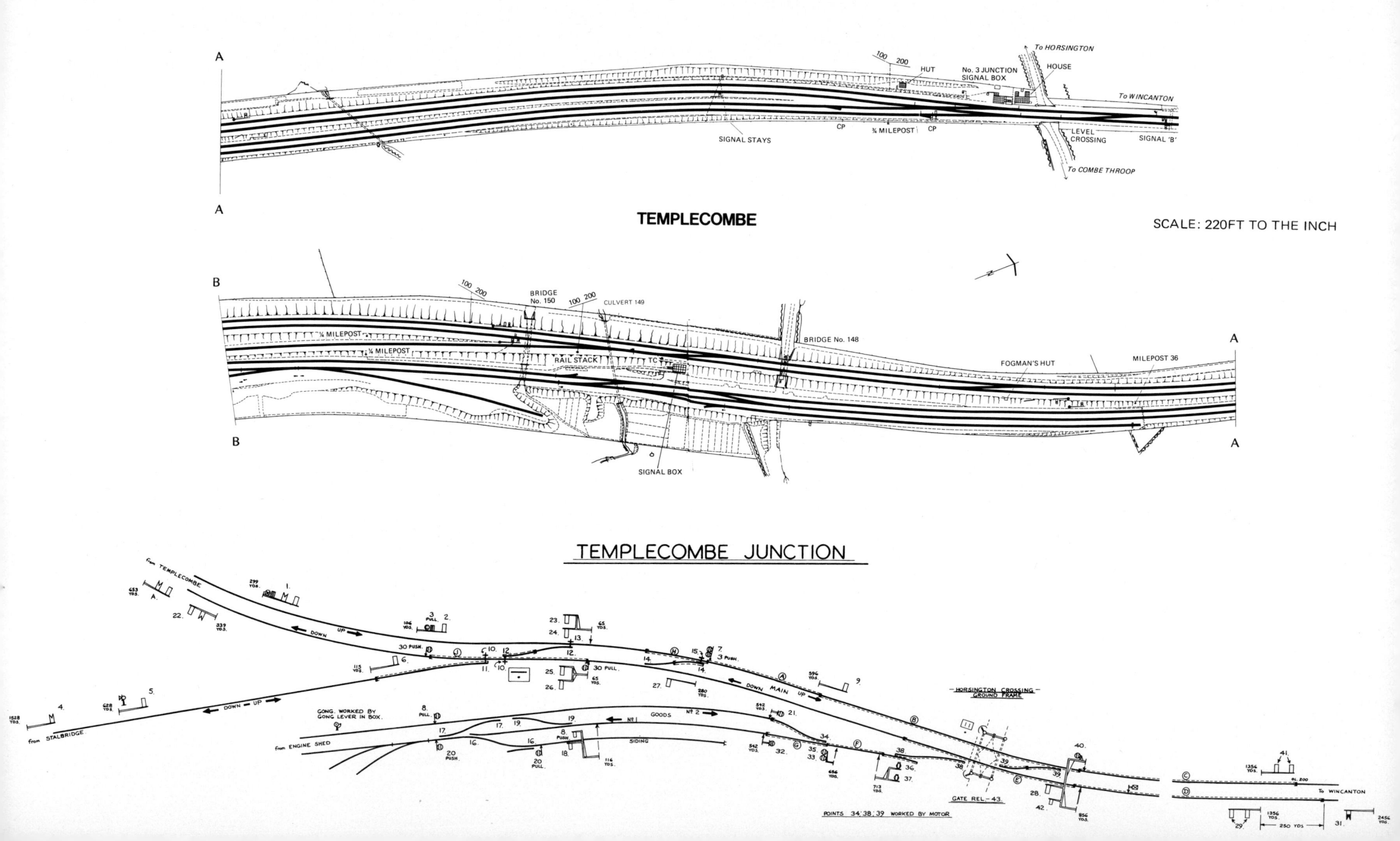

TEMPLECOMBE

SCALE: 220FT TO THE INCH

To HORSINGTON
To WINCANTON
HOUSE
No. 3 JUNCTION SIGNAL BOX
HUT
100 200
LEVEL CROSSING
SIGNAL 'B'
CP ¾ MILEPOST CP
SIGNAL STAYS
To COMBE THROOP

BRIDGE No. 150
CULVERT 149
100 200
100 200
BRIDGE No. 148
¼ MILEPOST
¼ MILEPOST
RAIL STACK
TC
FOGMAN'S HUT
MILEPOST 36
SIGNAL BOX

TEMPLECOMBE JUNCTION

from TEMPLECOMBE
653 YDS.
299 YDS.
22.
339 YDS.
DOWN UP
3. PULL. 2.
106 YDS.
23.
24.
65 YDS.
30 PUSH.
6. 10. 12.
11. 10.
13.
115 YDS.
6.
25.
26.
65 YDS.
15.
14.
14.
7.
3 PUSH.
594 YDS.
9.
DOWN MAIN UP
HORSINGTON CROSSING GROUND FRAME
4.
1528 YDS.
from STALBRIDGE
628 YDS.
5.
DOWN UP
GONG. WORKED BY GONG LEVER IN BOX.
8. PULL.
from ENGINE SHED
17.
20 PUSH.
16.
17.
19.
19.
8. PUSH.
No. 1
GOODS
No. 2
542 YDS.
21.
30 PULL.
280 YDS.
27.
542 YDS.
32.
35.
33.
34.
36.
37.
656 YDS.
713 YDS.
40.
28.
38.
38.
39.
39.
GATE REL. 43.
42.
856 YDS.
41.
1356 YDS.
RL. 200
To WINCANTON
1356 YDS.
250 YDS.
29.
31.
2456 YDS.
POINTS 34, 38, 39 WORKED BY MOTOR

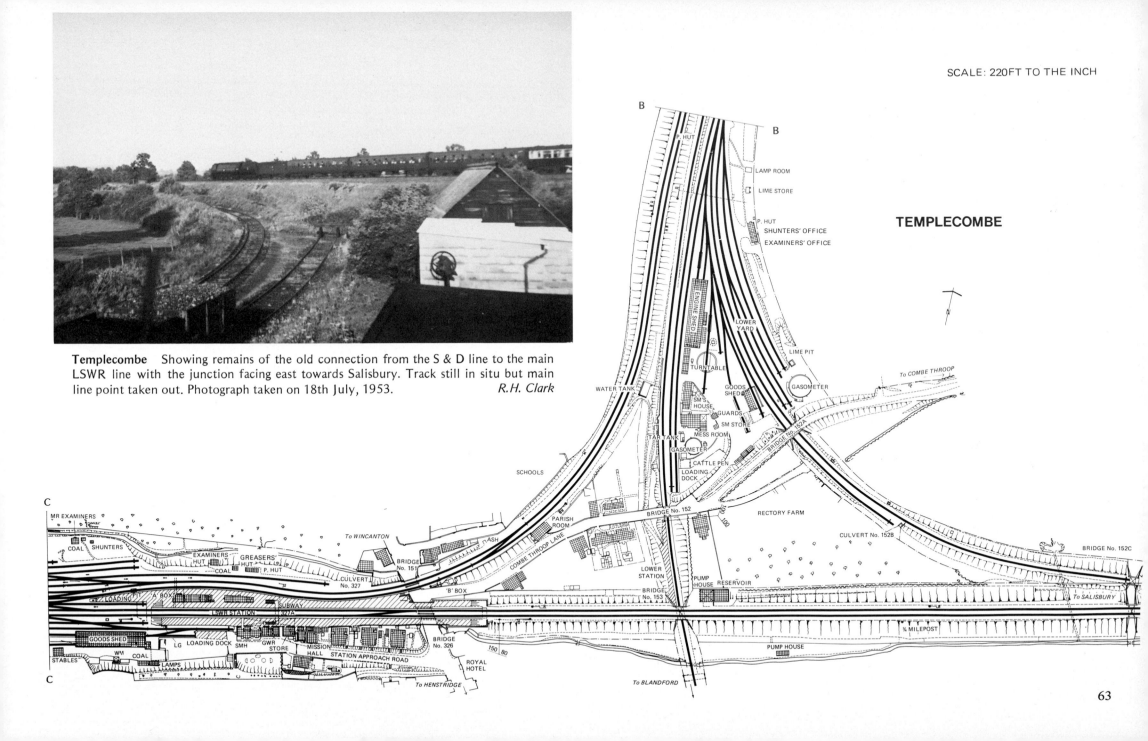

SCALE: 220FT TO THE INCH

TEMPLECOMBE

Templecombe Showing remains of the old connection from the S & D line to the main LSWR line with the junction facing east towards Salisbury. Track still in situ but main line point taken out. Photograph taken on 18th July, 1953.

R.H. Clark

B

B

P. HUT

LAMP ROOM

LIME STORE

P. HUT

SHUNTERS' OFFICE

EXAMINERS' OFFICE

ENGINE SHED

LOWER YARD

LIME PIT

TURNTABLE

To COMBE THROOP

WATER TANK

GOODS SHED

GASOMETER

SM'S HOUSE

GUARDS

SM STORE

TAR TANK

MESS ROOM

GASOMETER

CATTLE PEN

BRIDGE No. 152A

SCHOOLS

LOADING DOCK

PARISH ROOM

BRIDGE No. 152

RECTORY FARM

CULVERT No. 152B

100

C

MR EXAMINERS

COAL SHUNTERS

To WINCANTON

COMBE THROOP LANE

BRIDGE No. 152C

EXAMINERS' HUT

GREASERS' HUT

ASH

LOWER STATION

PUMP HOUSE

RESERVOIR

COAL

P. HUT

BRIDGE No. 151

CULVERT No. 327

'B' BOX

BRIDGE No. 153

To SALISBURY

LOADING

'A' BOX

SUBWAY 327A

LSWR STATION

½ MILEPOST

GOODS SHED

LG LOADING DOCK

SMH

GWR STORE

MISSION HALL

BRIDGE No. 326

150 80

PUMP HOUSE

STABLES

WM COAL

LAMPS

STATION APPROACH ROAD

ROYAL HOTEL

C

To HENSTRIDGE

To BLANDFORD

63

Templecombe Shed S&D class 7F 2-8-0 No. 53806 and BR Standard classes are present on 3rd July, 1961. The truncated eastern spur to the left of the LSWR line passes to the left of the goods shed and under the Combe Throop road bridge. The single line to the Lower Platform and Blandford is nearest the camera.

R.C. Riley

Templecombe Shed A close up of Templecombe shed with 0-6-0 No. 43436 standing outside.
Photomatic

Templecombe Shed 0-6-0 No. 43248 and another unidentified member of the same class stand in Templecombe shed sidings at the site of the former Dorset Central Templecombe station. The modern brick built engine shed is in the background. *Photomatic*

Templecombe Junction 0-6-0 No. 3215 takes a Bristol—Bournemouth train out of the Upper station, with a BR class 4 ready to continue the journey to Bournemouth.
Ivo Peters

Templecombe A very early photo of the upper station showing the S & D line curving in on the left.
G. Judd collection

Templecombe Shed The unpretentious stone buildings of the old Dorset Central station master's house.
R. Atthill

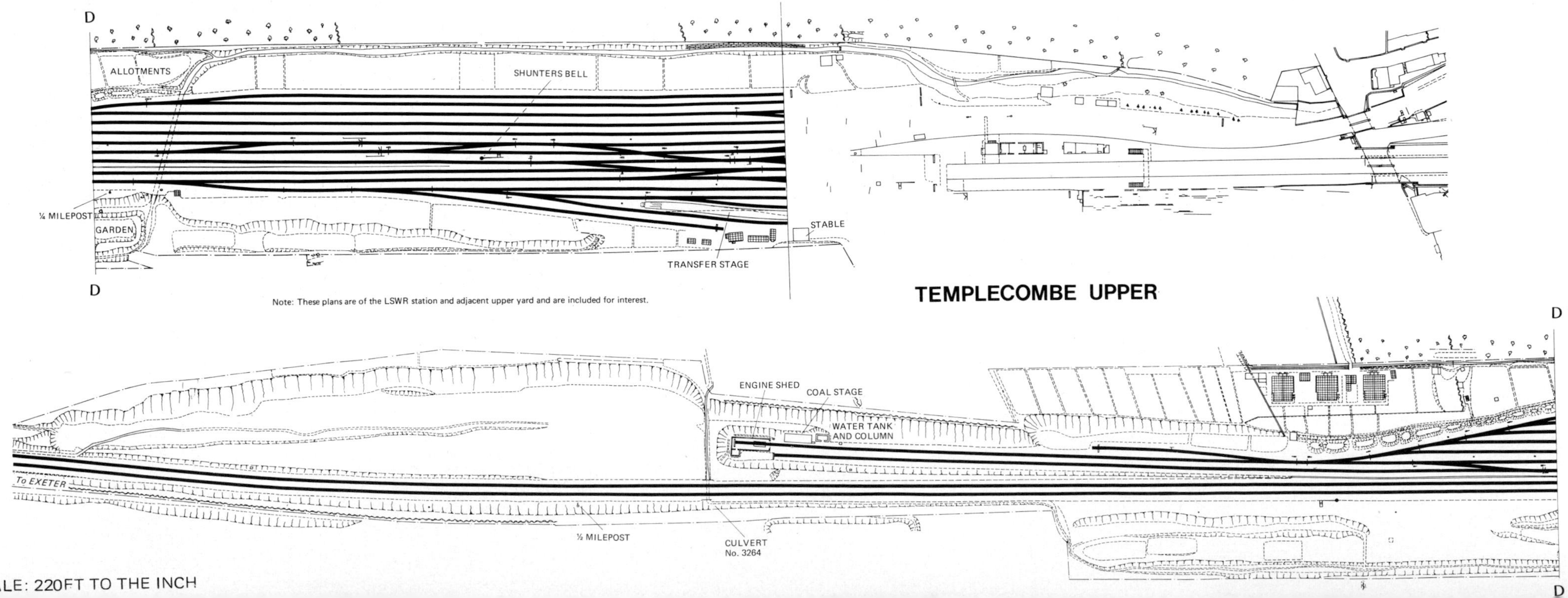

ALLOTMENTS

SHUNTERS BELL

¼ MILEPOST

GARDEN

STABLE

TRANSFER STAGE

Note: These plans are of the LSWR station and adjacent upper yard and are included for interest.

TEMPLECOMBE UPPER

ENGINE SHED

COAL STAGE

WATER TANK AND COLUMN

To EXETER

¼ MILEPOST

CULVERT No. 3264

SCALE: 220FT TO THE INCH

Templecombe Bridge carrying LSWR Waterloo — Exeter line in foreground and Templecombe Lower Platform is in the shadow between the two bridges. *R Atthill*

Templecombe Looking south. Lower Platform in foreground; LSWR bridge in background, July 1963. *M. O'Connor*

HENSTRIDGE

Opened: 31 August 1863
Closed: 7 March 1966 (to passengers)
              5 April 1965 (to goods)
Plan date: 1921

This was the smallest station on the line, the platform being only some 150 feet long. The station buildings contained a ground frame which controlled access to the small goods yard consisting of one siding. The ground frame and siding were taken out of use on 6th July, 1965.

Henstridge   Looking south.

Lens of Sutton

HENSTRIDGE

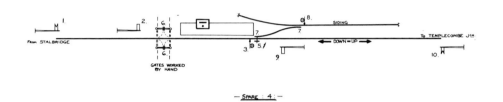

HENSTRIDGE

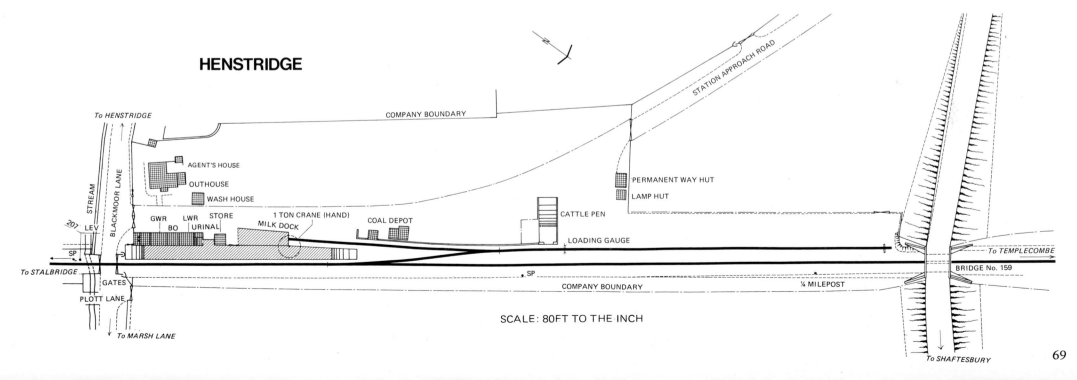

SCALE: 80 FT TO THE INCH

Stalbridge

A nice view of the station with the hand crane in the background.

R.C. Riley

STALBRIDGE

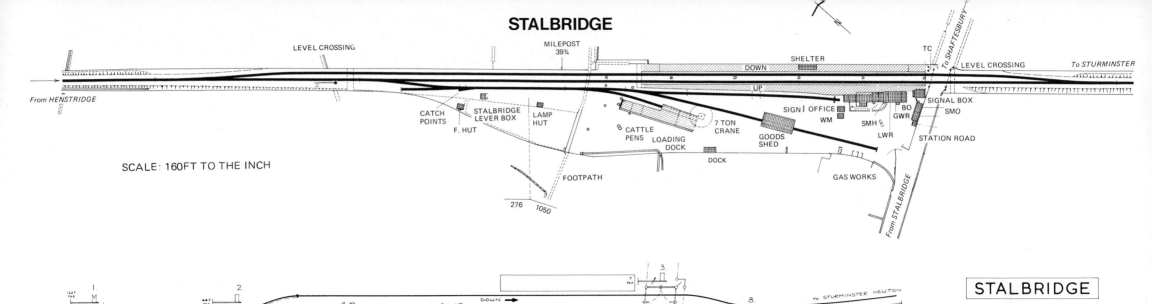

LEVEL CROSSING   MILEPOST 39¾   To SHAFTESBURY   TC   SHELTER   DOWN   To STURMINSTER   LEVEL CROSSING

UP

From HENSTRIDGE

CATCH POINTS   STALBRIDGE LEVER BOX   LAMP HUT   CATTLE PENS   7 TON CRANE   SIGN OFFICE   WM   SMH   BO GWR   SIGNAL BOX   SMO

F. HUT   LOADING DOCK   GOODS SHED   LWR   STATION ROAD

DOCK

SCALE: 160FT TO THE INCH

FOOTPATH   GAS WORKS   From STALBRIDGE

276   1050

STALBRIDGE

FROM TEMPLECOMBE JCN   UP   DOWN   To STURMINSTER NEWTON

POINTS 6. MOTOR WORKED

UP SIDINGS

SPARE - 10 : 11   GOODS SHED

16 – GATE STOPS
17 – GATE BOLT
18 – WICKETS

STALBRIDGE

Opened:	31 August 1863
Closed:	7 March 1966 (to passengers)
	5 April 1965 (to goods)
Plan date:	1921

The station buildings which were on the up platform here were built in brick and comprised from the northern end: station master's house, station offices and signal box. The latter was eighteen levers and was the first block post south of Templecombe. A long loop (of 1452 feet) was provided here for trains to cross, up trains as usual having the straight run through. A small goods yard was provided with the usual cattle pens and loading dock, and the long middle siding which crossed the main road at a gated crossing (not shown on above plan) gave access to a food store. All the sidings were taken out of use on 7th July, 1965 but the signal box remained to the end.

Stalbridge   The signal box and buildings on the up platform.   *P.I. Clarke*

Sturminster Newton An old view showing both platforms occupied. Note signalman holding out single line tablet. *Lens of Sutton*

Sturminster Newton A general view from the up platform; note the dip leading to the level crossing. *Lens of Sutton*

STURMINSTER NEWTON

Opened: 31 August 1863
Closed: 7 March 1966 (to passengers)
              5 April 1965 (to goods)
Plan date: 1921

The up platform, on which the station buildings were located, had a dip in the middle as will be seen from the photograph. This was because passengers had to cross the line on a wooden level crossing, there being no footbridge. The wooden signal box contained sixteen levers and stood at the eastern end of the up platform. In the commodious goods yard, sidings served cattle pens and a small brick built goods shed.

The lowering of the shunt signal No. 4 (see signalling plan) gave permission only to proceed as far as the up home signal (No. 15). If it was required to proceed further than this for shunting purposes, the signalman's permission needed to be obtained in advance.

Sturminster Newton A pre-nationalisation view of the station buildings and signal box. *Lens of Sutton*

STURMINSTER NEWTON

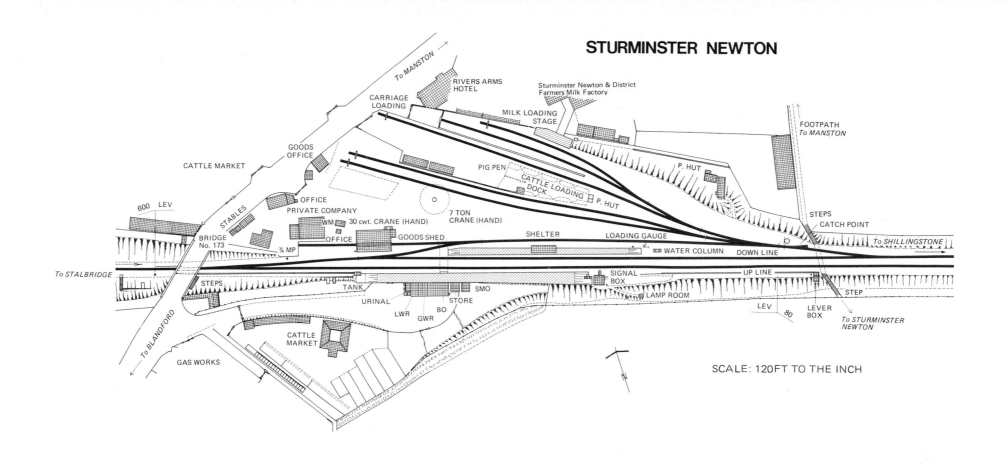

To MANSTON

RIVERS ARMS
HOTEL

Sturminster Newton & District
Farmers Milk Factory

CARRIAGE
LOADING

MILK LOADING
STAGE

FOOTPATH
To MANSTON

GOODS
OFFICE

CATTLE MARKET

PIG PEN

P. HUT

CATTLE LOADING
DOCK   P. HUT

600   LEV

STABLES

OFFICE
PRIVATE COMPANY

WM

30 cwt. CRANE (HAND)

7 TON
CRANE (HAND)

STEPS
CATCH POINT

BRIDGE
No. 173

¾ MP

OFFICE

GOODS SHED

SHELTER

LOADING GAUGE

To SHILLINGSTONE

WATER COLUMN   DOWN LINE

To STALBRIDGE

UP LINE

STEPS

TANK

URINAL

SMO

SIGNAL
BOX

LAMP ROOM

STEP

To BLANDFORD

LWR   GWR

STORE
BO

LEV   80

LEVER
BOX

To STURMINSTER
NEWTON

CATTLE
MARKET

GAS WORKS

N

SCALE: 120FT TO THE INCH

STURMINSTER NEWTON

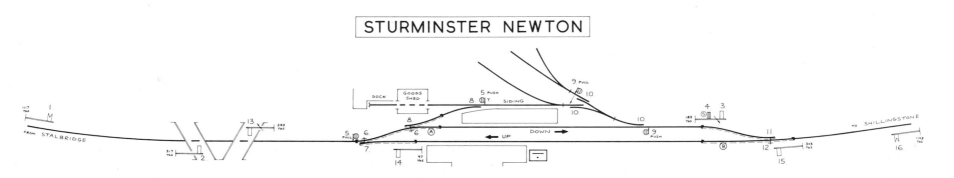

1117
Yds   1   M

FROM STALBRIDGE

13

243
Yds

DOCK

GOODS
SHED

5 PUSH

8

Y SIDING

9 PULL

10

4   3

183
Yds

To SHILLINGSTONE

317
Yds

8

5
PULL   6

6

A

10

10

9
PUSH

11

B

1163
Yds
16

14

2

7

UP   DOWN

12

15

57
Yds

313
Yds

TYER'S Nº 6 TABLET INSTRUMENTS

73

Sturminster Newton   In this charming 1961 view the pronounced dip in the up platform can clearly be seen.
R.C. Riley

Sturminster Newton   The west face of the building in 1965.   *M. O'Connor*

Sturminster Newton   The wooden signal box of LSWR design.   *M. O'Connor*

Sturminster Newton   The signal box, showing the tablet catching apparatus.   *R.C. Riley*

Shillingstone The station buildings seen from the down platform, c. 1910.
OPC Collection

SHILLINGSTONE

Opened: 31 August 1863
Closed: 7 March 1966 (to passengers)
5 April 1965 (to goods)
Plan date: 1923

Shillingstone possessed a very attractive garden on the up platform on which were located also the brick buildings. These carried an ornate awning — unusual for the southern end of the line. At the northern end of the up platform was the small sixteen lever wooden signal box beyond which there was a compact goods yard; this yard was closed on 5th April, 1965.

Shillingstone The west face of the station building. *M. O'Connor*

Shillingstone The up platform with signal box beyond. Note the Engineers' motorised trolley standing outside the box.
R.C. Riley

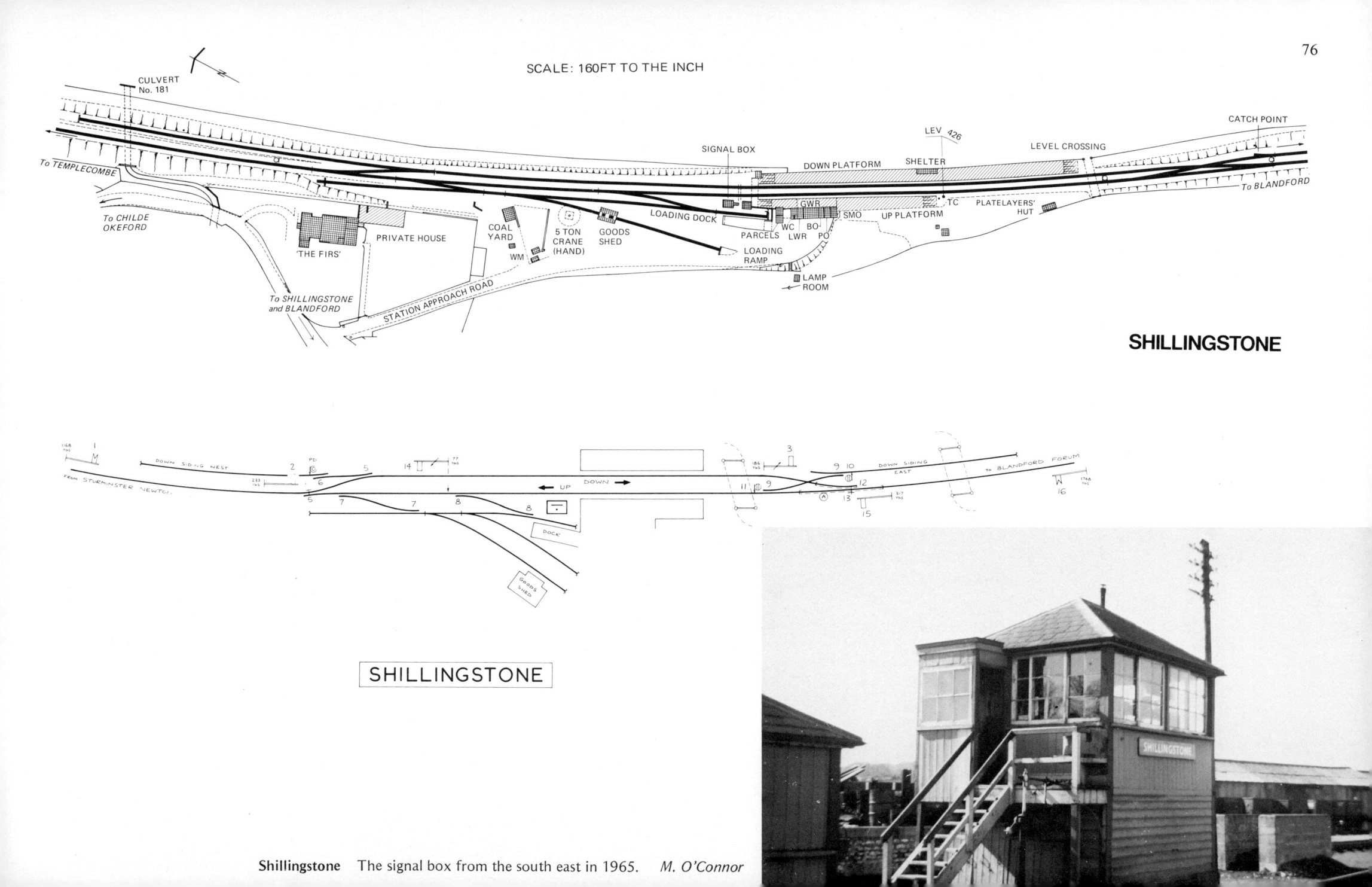

SCALE: 160FT TO THE INCH

76

CULVERT No. 181

CATCH POINT

SIGNAL BOX

LEV 426

LEVEL CROSSING

To TEMPLECOMBE

DOWN PLATFORM

SHELTER

To BLANDFORD

To CHILDE OKEFORD

LOADING DOCK

GWR

SMO

UP PLATFORM

TC

PLATELAYERS' HUT

'THE FIRS'

PRIVATE HOUSE

COAL YARD

5 TON CRANE (HAND)

GOODS SHED

PARCELS

WC LWR

BO PO

WM

LOADING RAMP

To SHILLINGSTONE and BLANDFORD

STATION APPROACH ROAD

LAMP ROOM

SHILLINGSTONE

DOWN SIDING WEST

FROM STURMINSTER NEWTON

UP DOWN

DOWN SIDING EAST

To BLANDFORD FORUM

DOCK

GOODS SHED

SHILLINGSTONE

Shillingstone The signal box from the south east in 1965. *M. O'Connor*

Stourpaine & Durweston Halt   Looking towards Blandford Forum; note the lamp.
OPC collection

Opened: 9 July 1928
Closed: 17 September 1956
Plan date: 1921

Half a mile to the north of Stourpaine Halt, a small signal box controlled a crossing loop which broke up the 5½ mile block section from Sturminster Newton to Blandford Forum. The straight up loop was signalled in both directions, and latterly it was only on days of heavy traffic that the box was switched in to circuit and the loops used for crossing trains. The down loop was removed and the signal box closed on 18th December, 1951.

Stourpaine & Durweston Halt was a simple concrete structure 120 feet long situated on the down side of the line. It possessed only a small shelter and had a short life, opening in 1928 and closing in 1956.

Between Stourpaine and Blandford and half a mile north of Blandford was the site of Milldown crossing; a ground frame and associated siding were situated here during the First World War serving a prisoner-of-war camp.

STOURPAINE & DURWESTON HALT

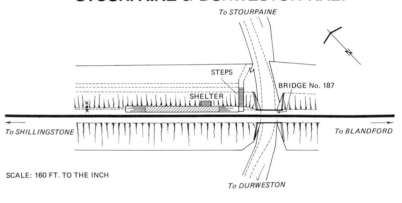

SCALE: 160 FT. TO THE INCH

STOURPAINE

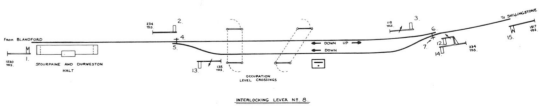

Stourpaine & Durweston Halt   The SR's influence is clearly seen in the use of standardised concrete components to reduce cost.
OPC Collection

BLANDFORD FORUM

Opened: 31 August 1863
Closed: 7 March 1966 (to passengers)
6 January 1969 (to goods)
Renaming: 'Blandford' until 21st September, 1953
This station replaced the first station 'Blandford St. Mary' which was opened on 1st November, 1860 and closed when the second station was opened.
Plan date: 1923

A large brick building with stone facings was provided on the up platform together with a commodious canopy. The down platform was dominated by the tall twenty seven lever signal box which controlled the extensive layout provided here. This replaced an earlier box on the up platform in 1893 and was itself destroyed by fire during a thunder-storm in 1906. The single line from Templecombe Jc. now became double for the next eight miles to Corfe Mullen. A useful goods yard was laid out on the down side together with goods shed and the usual cattle pens and loading docks.

Just south of the station adjacent to the pump house siding a double junction was provided to the Army Camp at Blandford but this had a very short existence being opened on 12th January, 1919, out of use by 1921 and removed during December 1928!

Blandford Forum An interesting early view showing the original signal box on the up platform, replaced in 1893. *OPC Collection*

BLANDFORD

SCALE: 215FT TO THE INCH

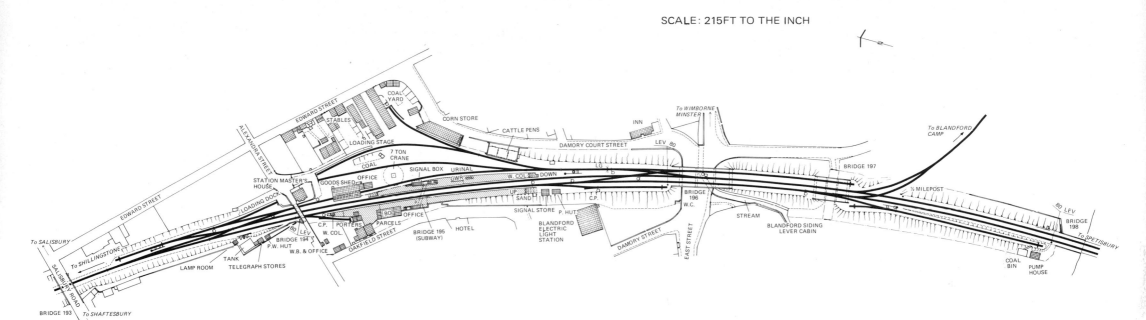

BLANDFORD

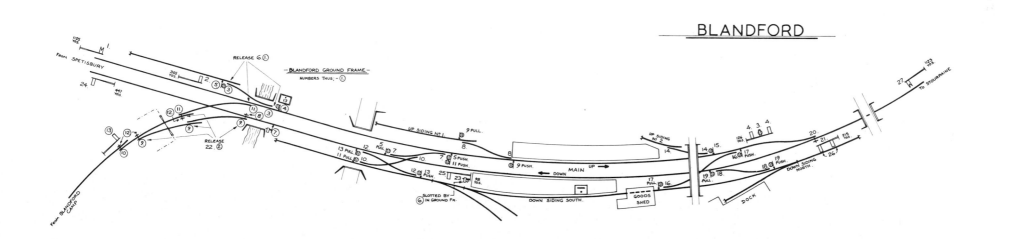

Blandford Forum c.1900 — note the shunting horse. A Fowler 0-6-0 stands on a goods train. *R. Atthill*

Blandford Forum An early view looking towards Spetisbury with the goods shed in foreground. *Lens of Sutton*

Blandford Forum The west face of the signal box. *M. O'Connor*

Blandford Forum The signal box and goods shed. *M.J. Palmer*

Blandford Forum   Looking towards Templecombe; yard crane at right.

Lens of Sutton

Blandford Forum   The well preserved station in 1961.

R.C. Riley

Charlton Marshall Halt   Two views of the very basic facilities provided here.

OPC collection

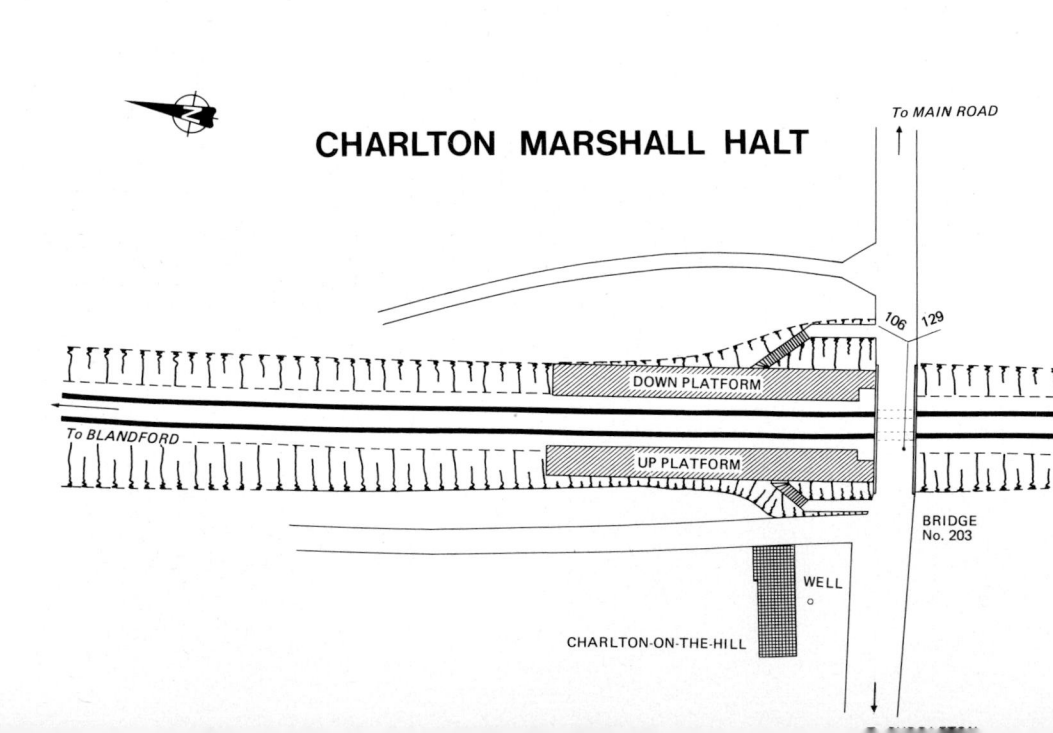

CHARLTON MARSHALL HALT

CHARLTON MARSHALL HALT

Opened: 5 July 1928
Closed: 17 September 1956
Plan date: c. 1930's

This simple halt was, like Stourpaine & Durweston, in existence only for a short time, opening in 1928 and closing in 1956.

SCALE: 80FT TO THE INCH

5295

Spetisbury   A pre-1901 view of the station; note the disc and crossbar signal, one of the last remaining on the line which was removed on 16th April, 1901.

R. Atthill

Opened: 1 November 1860 (Opened as 'Spetisbury')
Closed: 17 September 1956
            Unstaffed from 13 August 1934
Plan date: 1923

    A mile and a half beyond Charlton Marshall lay Spetisbury Halt. This was originally a station with a signal box that broke the section from Blandford Forum to Bailey Gate; the box closed in 1952 and the halt itself in 1956.

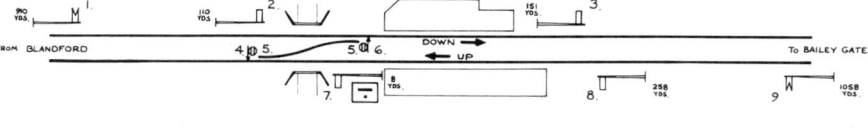

SPETISBURY

Spetisbury   Seen here in 1961, five years after closure.   *OPC Collection*

CROSS-OVER POINTS. (Nº 5) ELECTRICALLY LOCKED
BY BAILEY GATE AND BLANDFORD WHEN SPETISBURY
SWITCHED OUT, AND UNLOCKED WHEN BOX OPENED
AS BLOCK POST.

SCALE: 120FT TO THE INCH

SPETISBURY

Opened:	1 November 1860 (as 'Sturminster Marshall')
Closed:	7 March 1966 (to passengers)
	5 April 1965 (to public goods traffic)
Renaming:	'Sturminster Marshall' until November, 1863
	Presumably renamed to avoid confusion with 'Sturminster Newton'
Plan date:	1923 (opened 31 August 1863)

Following the opening of Broadstone direct line in 1884/5 and until the provision of a signal box at Corfe Mullen in 1905 this was the physical junction for Wimborne and Broadstone.

A neat brick building was provided on the down platform here together with a single wooden hut acting as a waiting room on the up side. A small wooden signal box of twenty four levers with a block switch controlled the quite extensive layout. The major traffic handled was milk from the United Dairies' sidings which was sent to London, initially via Wimborne but following closure of the direct line to Wimborne in 1933, the milk was re-routed via Templecombe.

Bailey Gate   Looking towards Broadstone.
OPC collection

Bailey Gate   Another view towards Broadstone.   *R. Atthill*

Bailey Gate   A 1961 view.   *R.C. Riley*

BAILEY GATE

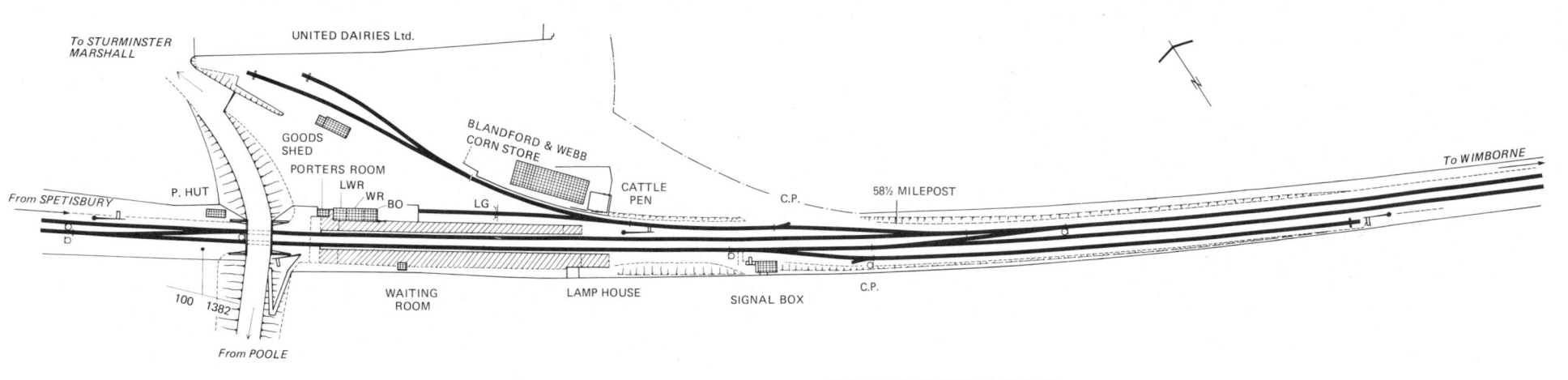

To STURMINSTER MARSHALL

UNITED DAIRIES Ltd.

GOODS SHED

PORTERS ROOM

BLANDFORD & WEBB CORN STORE

CATTLE PEN

To WIMBORNE

P. HUT

From SPETISBURY

LWR

WR BO

LG

C.P.

58½ MILEPOST

D

100 1382

From POOLE

WAITING ROOM

LAMP HOUSE

SIGNAL BOX

C.P.

SCALE: 160FT TO THE INCH

BAILEY GATE

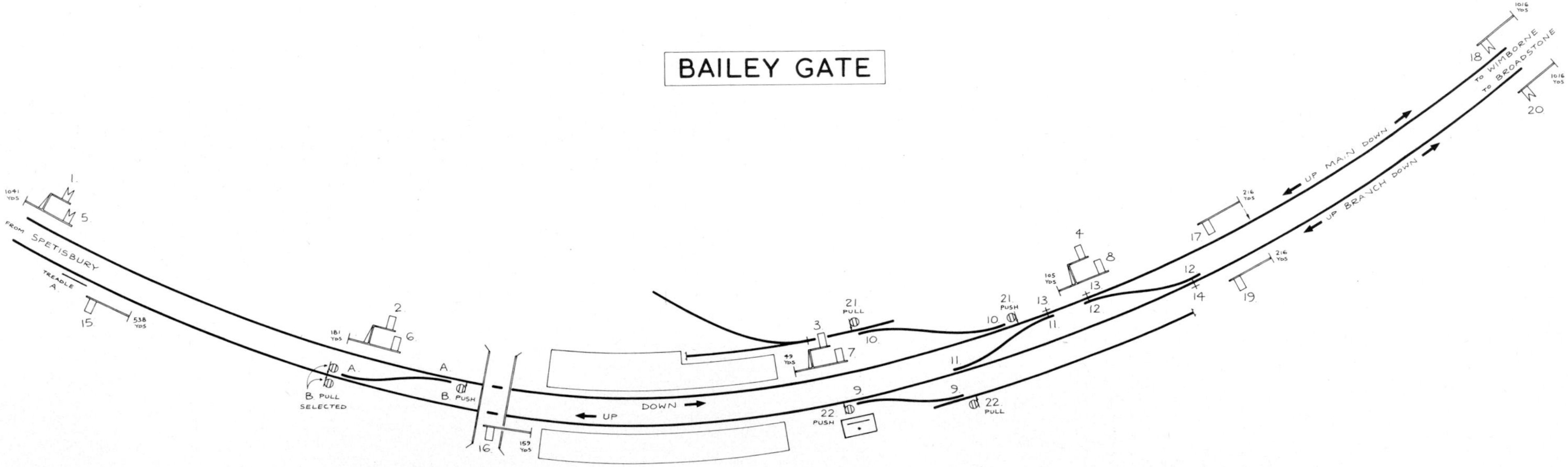

FROM SPETISBURY

TO WIMBORNE

TO BROADSTONE

UP MAIN DOWN

UP BRANCH DOWN

TREADLE A

DOWN

UP

LAYOUT AS FROM 1885 TO 1905

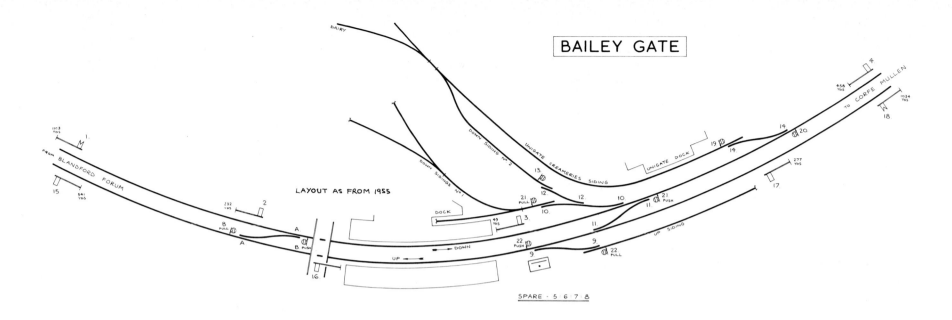

BAILEY GATE

LAYOUT AS FROM 1955

FROM BLANDFORD FORUM

TO CORFE MULLEN

SPARE · 5 · 6 · 7 · 8

BAILEY GATE CROSSING

The signalling plan shown is pre-1923 as the signal box ceased to be a block post on 5th April, 1923. The two sidings on the down side, 'Admiralty sidings', remained with access from the Corfe Mullen end only and were eventually removed before 1955. The ground frame at the crossing was itself closed on 7th May, 1968 when the line from Broadstone to Blandford was converted to a siding until its eventual closure on 6th January, 1969.

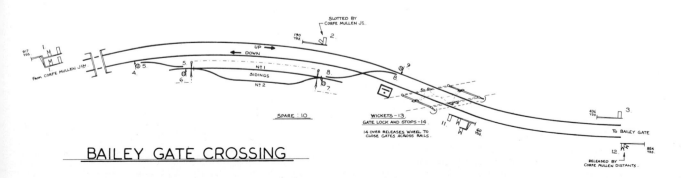

SLOTTED BY
CORFE MULLEN JS.

UP
DOWN

From CORFE MULLEN JCN.

No.1
SIDINGS
No.2

SPARE : 10

WICKETS - 13.
GATE LOCK AND STOPS - 14
14 OVER RELEASES WHEEL TO
CLOSE GATES ACROSS RAILS.

RELEASED BY
CORFE MULLEN DISTANTS.

TO BAILEY GATE

BAILEY GATE CROSSING

Bailey Gate Crossing

The signal box controlling the crossing over the Dorchester—Wimborne road.

P.I. Clarke

CORFE MULLEN

To BERE REGIS

To BERE REGIS

ST. HUBERT'S CHURCH

To WIMBORNE

To BAILEY GATE
FOOTPATH

CORFE MULLEN
LEVEL CROSSING
¼ MILEPOST

· TC WELL

TC

CORFE MULLEN
JUNC.
SIGNAL BOX

BRIDGE 223

To BROADSTONE

CULVERT NO. 222
(4' 0" DIAM.)

To POOLE

105 300

To BROADSTONE

1243 375

375 85

85 105

To BROADSTONE

SCALE: 130FT TO THE INCH

CORFE MULLEN JUNCTION
(c.1930)

From BAILEY GATE

BAILEY GATE CROSSING
DOWN HOME.

DOWN

UP

23. - GATE STOPS AND LOCKS.
24. - WICKETS.

F.B. 9.

TREADLE
A

THREADLE
B

MAIN

BRANCH

TREADLE
C

To WIMBORNE
LOOP

To BROADSTONE
JCN.

15 AND 16 :- BRIDGE INDICATORS

BAILEY GATE CROSSING
UP DISTANTS.

SPARE : 14 : 22 :

The signal box.   P.I. Clarke

CORFE   MULLEN
(c. 1950)

CORFE MULLEN

BAILEY GATE

DOWN

UP

SLOTTED BY BAILEY
GATE CROSSING

CARTERS SIDING

13R

12 13

UP MAIN DOWN

BROADSTONE

GATE BOLT & STOPS : 23.

WICKETS : 24.

SPARES : 1. 5. 6. 7. 8. 14. 15. 16. 18. 19. 22.

CORFE MULLEN JUNCTION

Plan date: 1923

Corfe Mullen Junction was where the original line to Wimborne (closed in 1933 except for a mile long stub to Carter's siding near Corfe Mullen) bore away left from the direct line to Broadstone, opened in 1884/5. A twenty four lever signal box, opened in 1905, controlled the junction and the points between the double line from Blandford and the single line onwards to Broadstone. Before the opening of the junction there had been gate boxes both here and at Bailey Gate crossing which signalled trains running on the then single lines. The section of line to Carter's siding was closed on 19th September, 1959, although it was retained for wagon storage for another ten years. The signal box closed on 7th May, 1968.

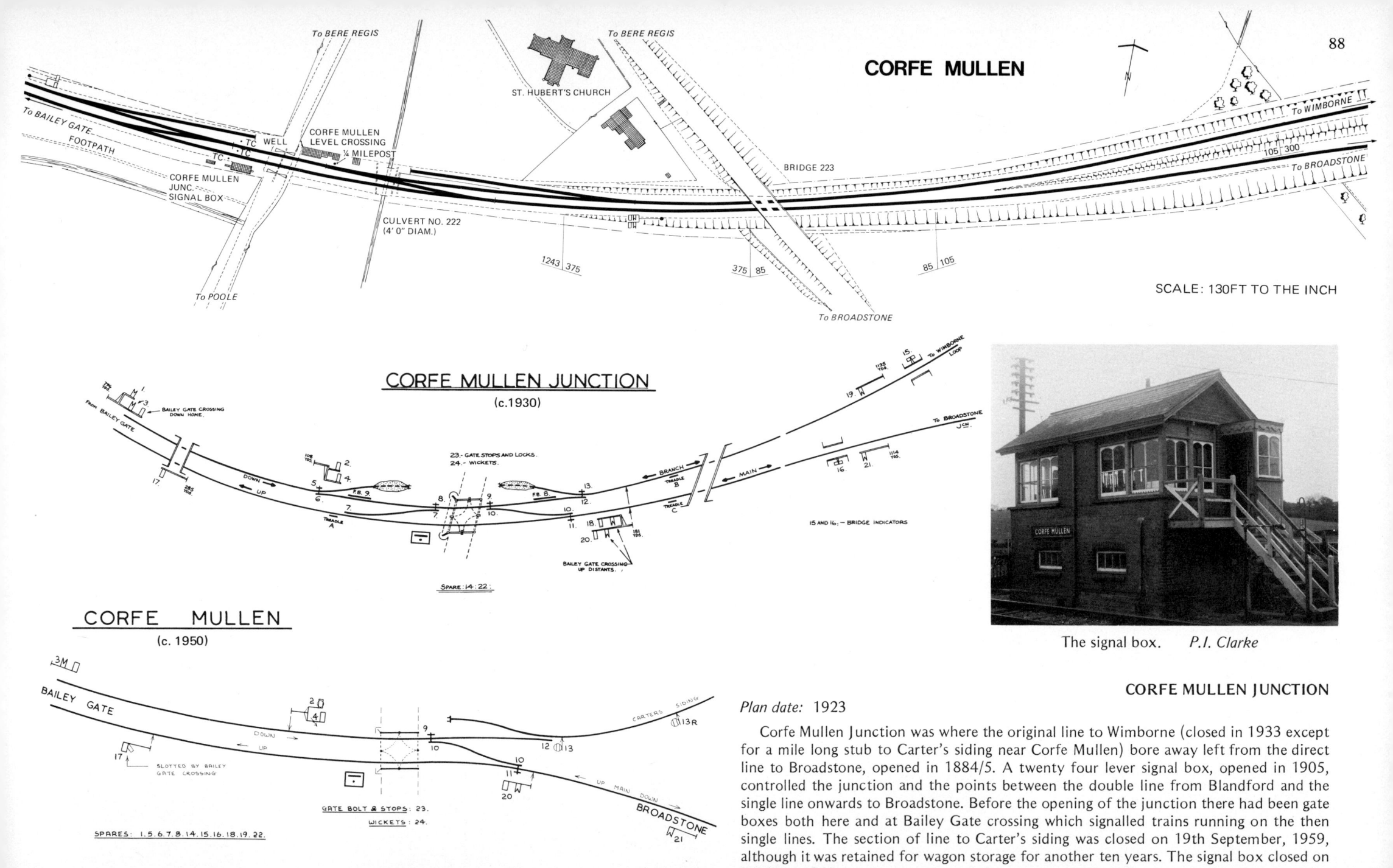

Opened:	5 July 1928
Closed:	19 September 1956
Plan date:	c. 1930's

Although the inhabitants of Corfe Mullen village had asked for a station to be provided when the line was opened in 1884 it was not provided until 1928, and like the other halts south of Templecombe closed in 1956 — a brief existence indeed!

Corfe Mullen Halt   Only the bare essentials!

OPC collection

CORFE MULLEN HALT

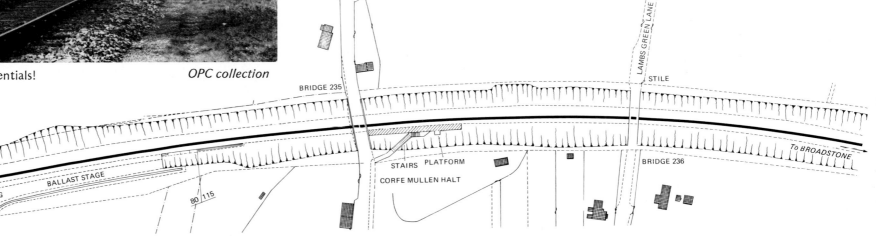

CARTER'S SIDING

SCALE: 160FT TO THE INCH

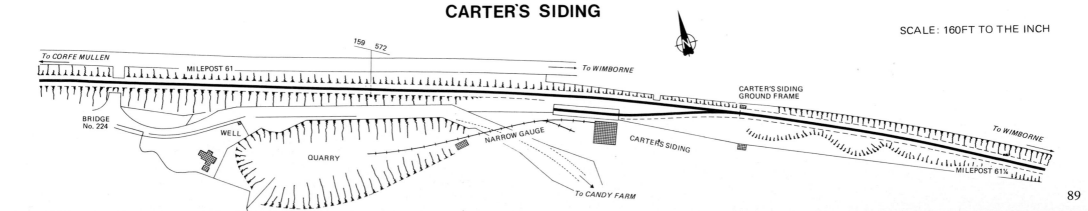

Opened: 1 June 1847 (original LSWR opening)
          2 December 1872 (opened to S & DR trains)
Renamings: 'New Poole Junction' until January 1876
          'Poole Junction' until July 1883
          'Poole Junction & Broadstone' until January 1887
          'Broadstone & New Poole Junction' until 15 February 1889
          'Broadstone Junction' until July 1929
          'Broadstone (Dorset)' until 1956
          'Broadstone' thereafter
          (The first three titles and dates are 'first or last' appearances in timetables)
Plan date: 1923

At Broadstone the Somerset and Dorset ended and trains ran on the LSWR to Poole and Bournemouth. Until 1874 trains ran to what later became Hamworthy Goods on the west side of Poole Harbour. However following opening of a new direct line from Broadstone to Holes Bay Junction near Poole, trains used the new eastern side platforms from 1874 onwards. A thirty two lever LSWR signal box controlled the junction and associated sidings. The box originally contained a 33 lever frame (see earlier diagram) but this was replaced after the Second World War by an 'A2' frame of 32 levers which came from the wartime Lockerley sidings box on the Salisbury—Romsey line.

Although this was, in the old days, a busy and important interchange station, passengers were provided with more than ample platform space, and conversely the very minimum of covered accommodation. The station buildings were squat, single storey, and mostly timber-covered brick structures which boasted lanky and elaborate chimney stacks, which were fashionable at the period.

The station was, however, strategically placed geographically, and handled the S & D trains, the local trains of the LSWR from Salisbury and Brockenhurst (via Wimborne), and, until the opening of the Holes Bay curve in 1893, the whole service between Waterloo, Dorchester, and Weymouth.

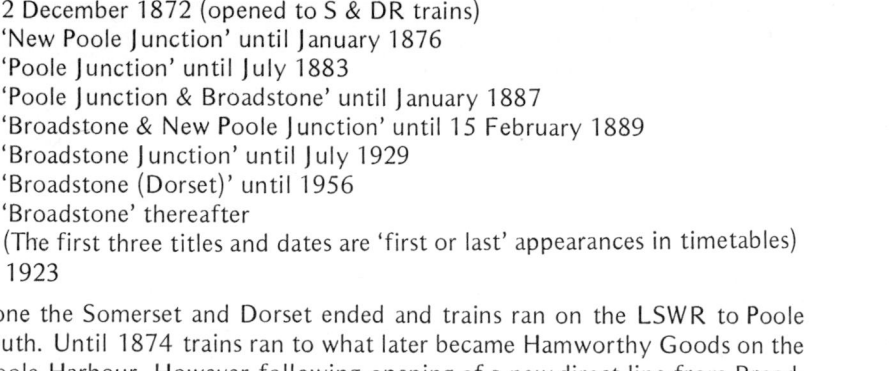

Broadstone   The station nameboard.   *OPC Collection*

BROADSTONE

SCALE: 190FT TO THE INCH

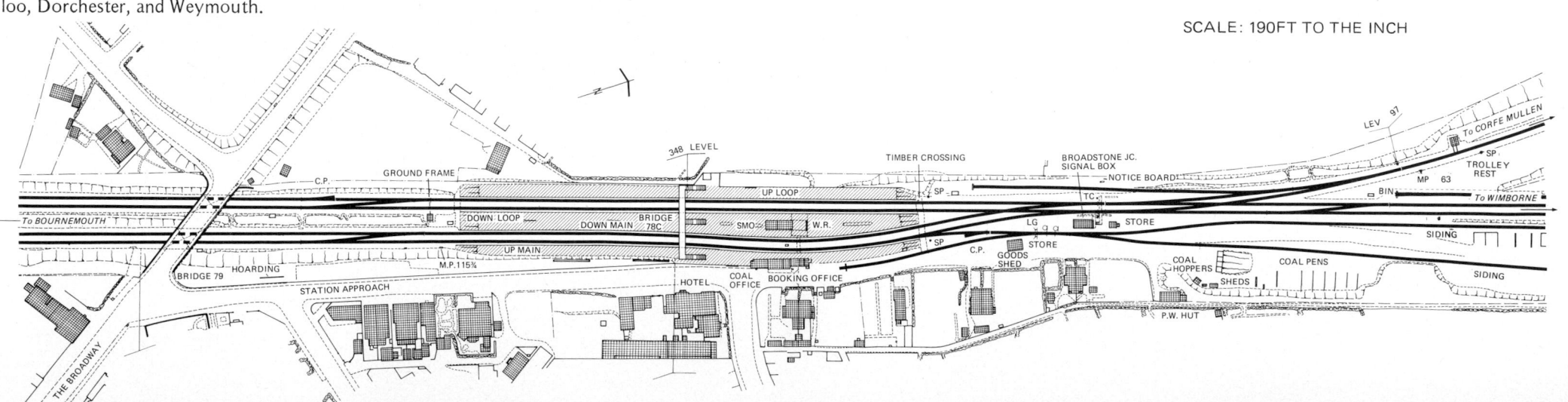

Broadstone   The outside of the station, downside, photographed in May 1940.

G.W. Puntis

Broadstone   The 'running-in' sign on the up main platform.

C.L. Caddy

Broadstone   The signal box photographed in 1965.

C.L. Caddy

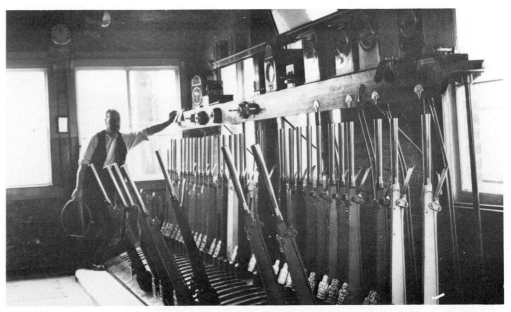

Broadstone   Inside the LSWR signal box in July 1939 showing the original lever frame.

G.W. Puntis

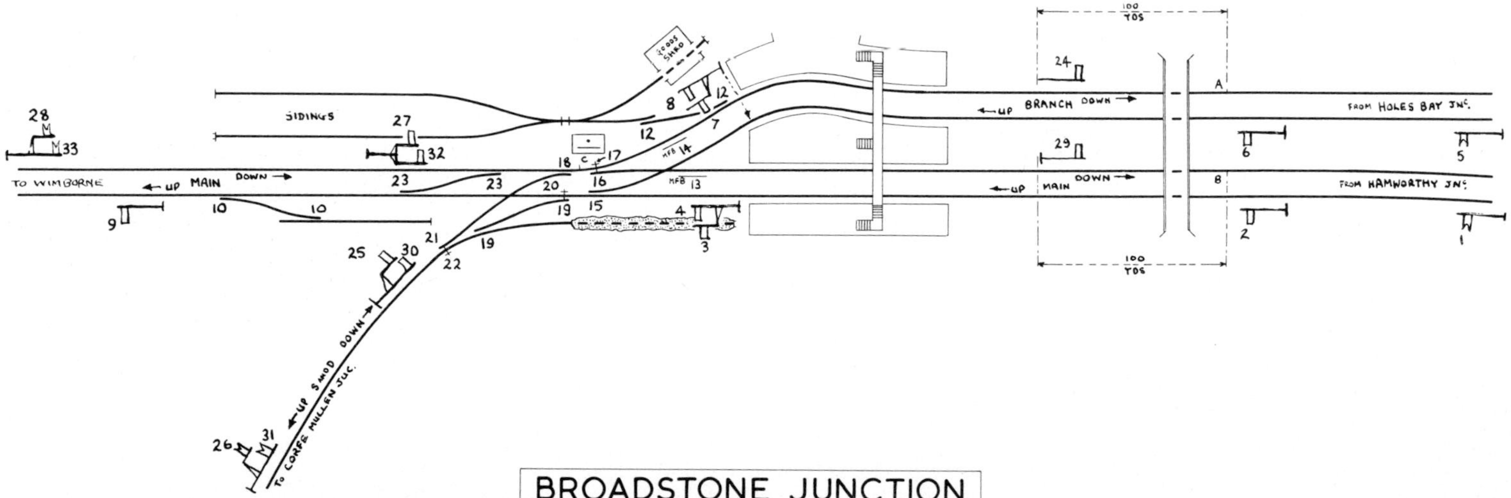

BROADSTONE JUNCTION

(c. 1893)

SPARE – 11

Nº 6 TABLET TO CORFE MULLEN
PREECE'S ONE WIRE BLOCK TO POOLE 'B' AND WIMBORNE

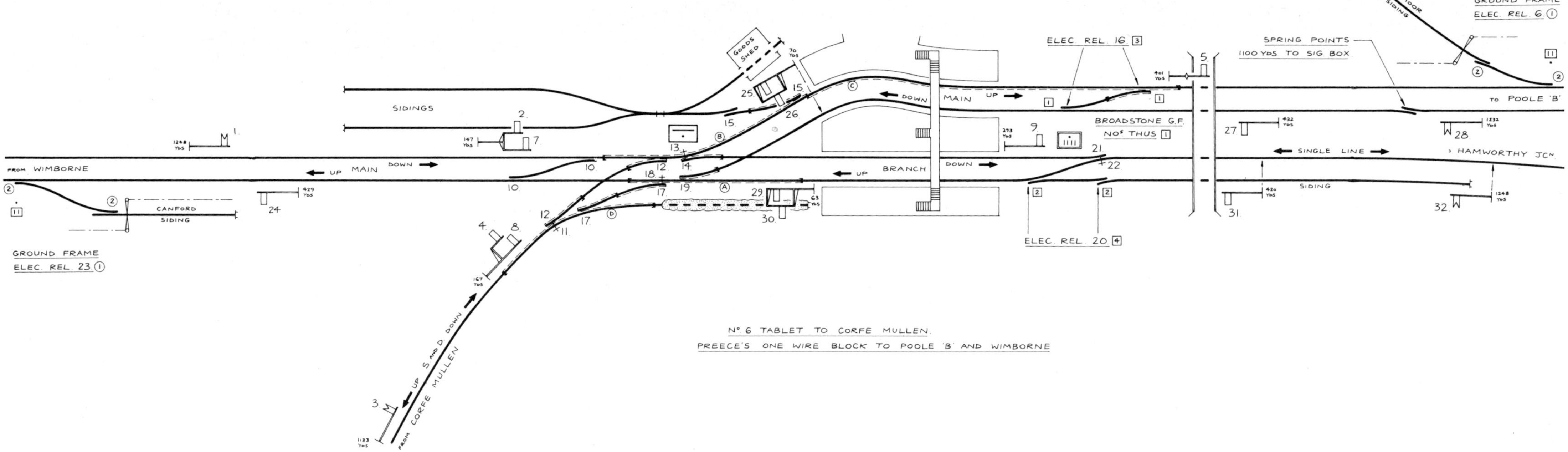

BROADSTONE

(c. 1960)

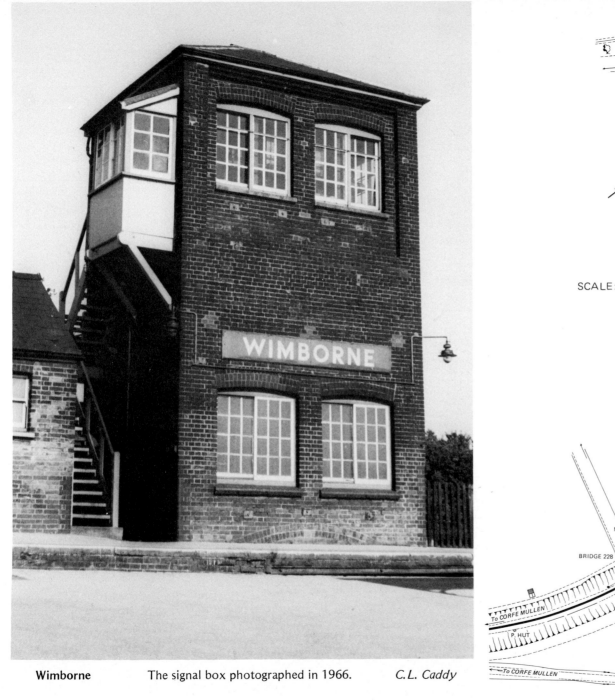

Wimborne   The signal box photographed in 1966.   *C.L. Caddy*

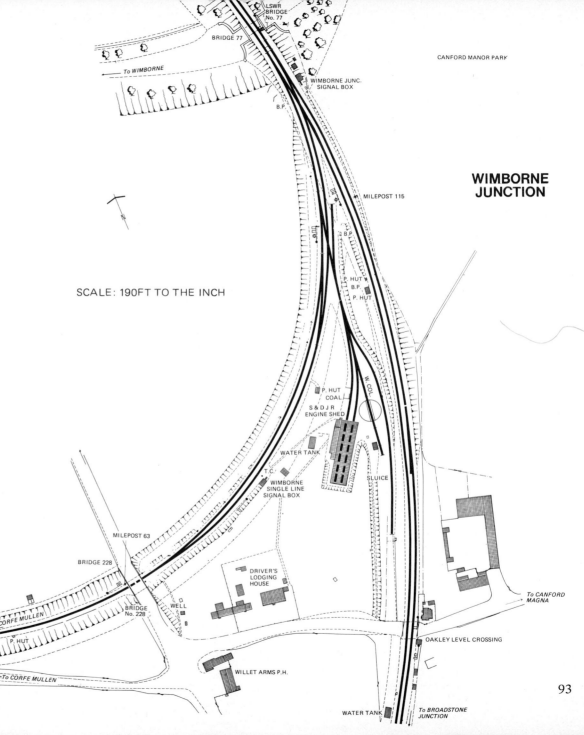

WIMBORNE JUNCTION

SCALE: 190FT TO THE INCH

LSWR BRIDGE No. 77

BRIDGE 77

CANFORD MANOR PARK

To WIMBORNE

WIMBORNE JUNC. SIGNAL BOX

B.P.

MILEPOST 115

B.P.

P. HUT

B.P.

P. HUT

P. HUT

COAL

W. COL.

S & D J R ENGINE SHED

WATER TANK

SLUICE

T.C.

WIMBORNE SINGLE LINE SIGNAL BOX

MILEPOST 63

BRIDGE 228

DRIVER'S LODGING HOUSE

To CORFE MULLEN

BRIDGE No. 228

WELL

To CANFORD MAGNA

To CORFE MULLEN

P. HUT

WILLET ARMS P.H.

OAKLEY LEVEL CROSSING

WATER TANK

To BROADSTONE JUNCTION

Wimborne   The station nameboard. *OPC Collection*

Wimborne   Looking towards Broadstone (1966). *C.L. Caddy*

WIMBORNE (LSWR)

Opened: 1 November 1860 (opened to S & DR trains)
Closed: 11 July 1920 (to S & D passenger trains)
              17 June 1933 (to S & D goods trains)
Plan date: 1923

From Corfe Mullen the Somerset and Dorset extended eastwards for almost another three miles to Wimborne Junction signal box, the last twenty three chains from that point into Wimborne station being LSWR property. This was the original main line but after the opening of the direct line from Corfe Mullen to Broadstone on 14th December, 1885 it became very much a branch and eventually lost its passenger service on 11th July, 1920. Milk trains continued until 28th February, 1932 and general freight until 17th June, 1933. After that date, as already recorded, the line was closed at the Wimborne end leaving a short siding to serve the clay pits at Carter's siding from the Corfe Mullen end.

Some 12 chains before the LSWR main line was reached the single line from Corfe Mullen became double; this junction was controlled by Wimborne Single Line signal box (closed in April 1928). In the 'vee' between the S & D line and the LSWR was a medium size engine shed complete with 44 foot turntable and water tank, and, as will be seen from the plan, set back from the shed, a drivers' hostel.

Wimborne Junction LSWR signal box closed in 1933 following the closure of the line from Corfe Mullen.

Wimborne   Towards Ringwood (1966). *C.L. Caddy*

Wimborne   BR Standard class 4 2-6-0 No. 76026 with a train for Broadstone. *P.I. Clarke*

Wimborne   The up buildings (1975).   *M. O'Connor*

Wimborne   The station in 1966, looking west.   *C.L. Caddy*

Wimborne   The goods shed viewed from the east (1975).   *M. O'Connor*

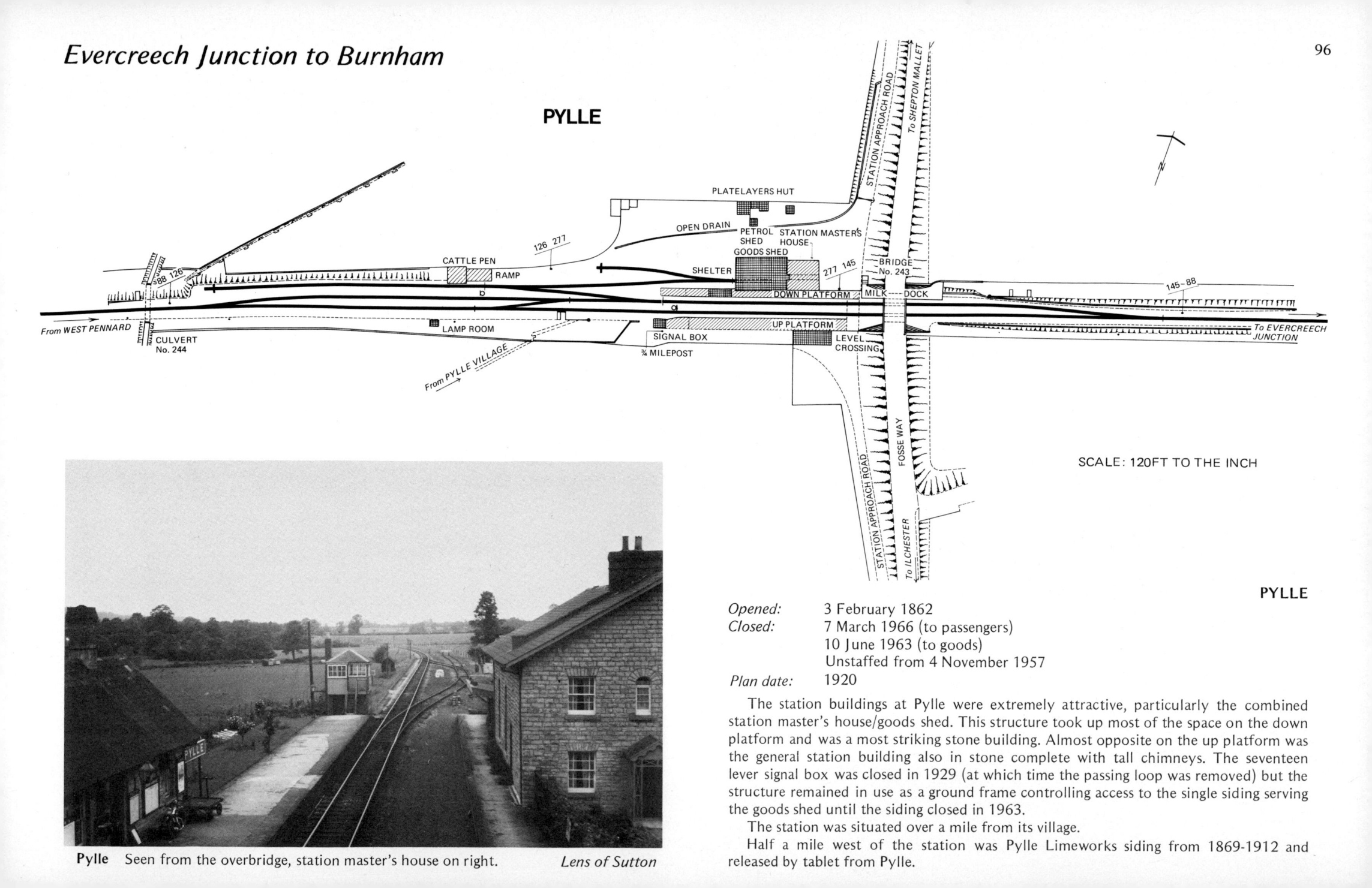

PYLLE

PLATELAYERS HUT

OPEN DRAIN

STATION APPROACH ROAD

To SHEPTON MALLET

126 277

PETROL STATION MASTER'S
SHED HOUSE
GOODS SHED

CATTLE PEN

88 126

RAMP

SHELTER

277 145

BRIDGE
No. 243

DOWN PLATFORM

MILK DOCK

145 – 88

From WEST PENNARD

CULVERT
No. 244

LAMP ROOM

SIGNAL BOX

UP PLATFORM

To EVERCREECH
JUNCTION

From PYLLE VILLAGE

¾ MILEPOST

LEVEL
CROSSING

FOSSE WAY

STATION APPROACH ROAD

To ILCHESTER

SCALE: 120FT TO THE INCH

PYLLE

Opened: 3 February 1862
Closed: 7 March 1966 (to passengers)
              10 June 1963 (to goods)
              Unstaffed from 4 November 1957
Plan date: 1920

The station buildings at Pylle were extremely attractive, particularly the combined station master's house/goods shed. This structure took up most of the space on the down platform and was a most striking stone building. Almost opposite on the up platform was the general station building also in stone complete with tall chimneys. The seventeen lever signal box was closed in 1929 (at which time the passing loop was removed) but the structure remained in use as a ground frame controlling access to the single siding serving the goods shed until the siding closed in 1963.

The station was situated over a mile from its village.

Half a mile west of the station was Pylle Limeworks siding from 1869-1912 and released by tablet from Pylle.

Pylle   Seen from the overbridge, station master's house on right.   *Lens of Sutton*

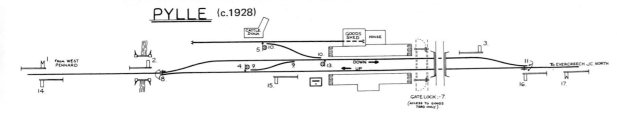

PYLLE (c.1928)

SPARE: 6.12.
8 AND 11; - 'ECONOMIC' LOCKS.

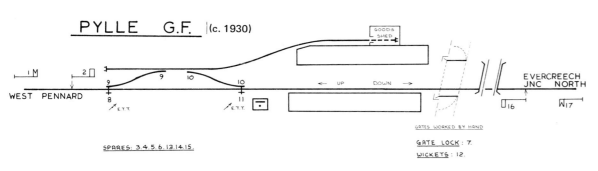

PYLLE G.F. (c. 1930)

SPARES: 3.4.5.6.13.14.15.

GATES WORKED BY HAND

GATE LOCK: 7.

WICKETS: 12.

Pylle The signal box had been reduced to a ground frame in 1929; it is seen here c. 1961.
Lens of Sutton

Pylle The station building.   *OPC collection*

Pylle The attractive frontage of the station master's house with goods shed behind.
OPC collection

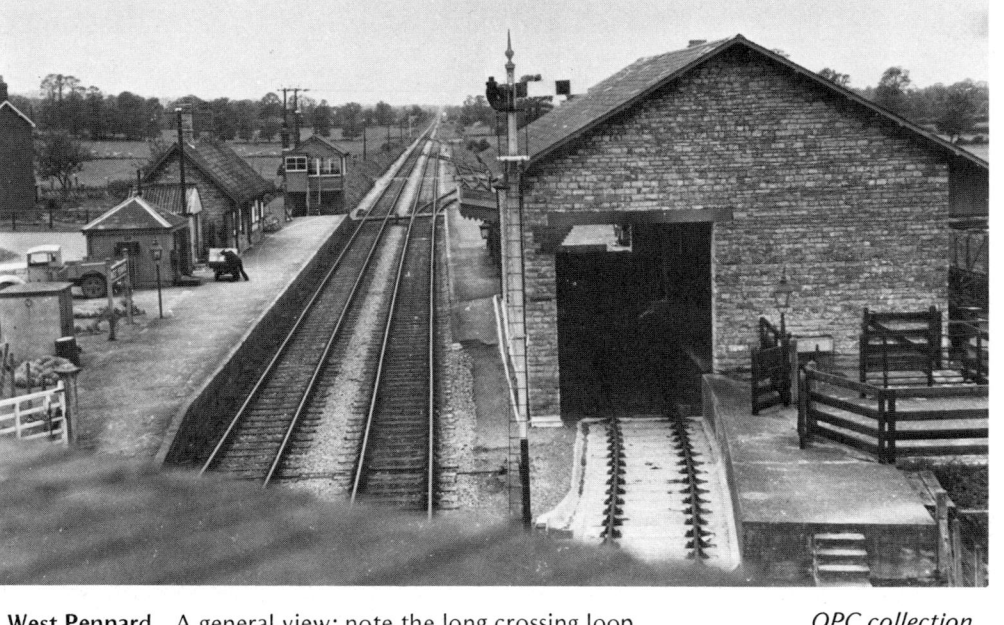

West Pennard   A general view; note the long crossing loop.   *OPC collection*

West Pennard   The neat station building.   *OPC collection*

WEST PENNARD

Opened: 3 February 1862
Closed: 7 March 1966 (to passengers)
                10 June 1963 (to goods)
                Unstaffed from 25 June 1962
Plan date: 1920

Almost at the foot of the four mile long bank which descended from Pylle with a ruling gradient of 1 in 86 stood West Pennard station. This station was situated some two miles from its village on a section of line that ran dead straight for four miles, quite unlike the main line from Evercreech Jc. to Bath which abounded in curves.

A large stone built goods shed was provided with access from a double ended siding which ran at the back of the short down platform. On this platform stood a large wooden shelter whilst opposite on the up platform stood the neat high-roofed stone building housing the booking office, waiting room and staff quarters.

An attractive wooden signal box on a stone base stood at the west end of the up platform. This twenty three lever box closed on 26th August, 1964 at which time the down loop line and all sidings were taken out of use.

West Pennard   Towards Evercreech Jc.   *OPC collection*

WEST PENNARD STATION

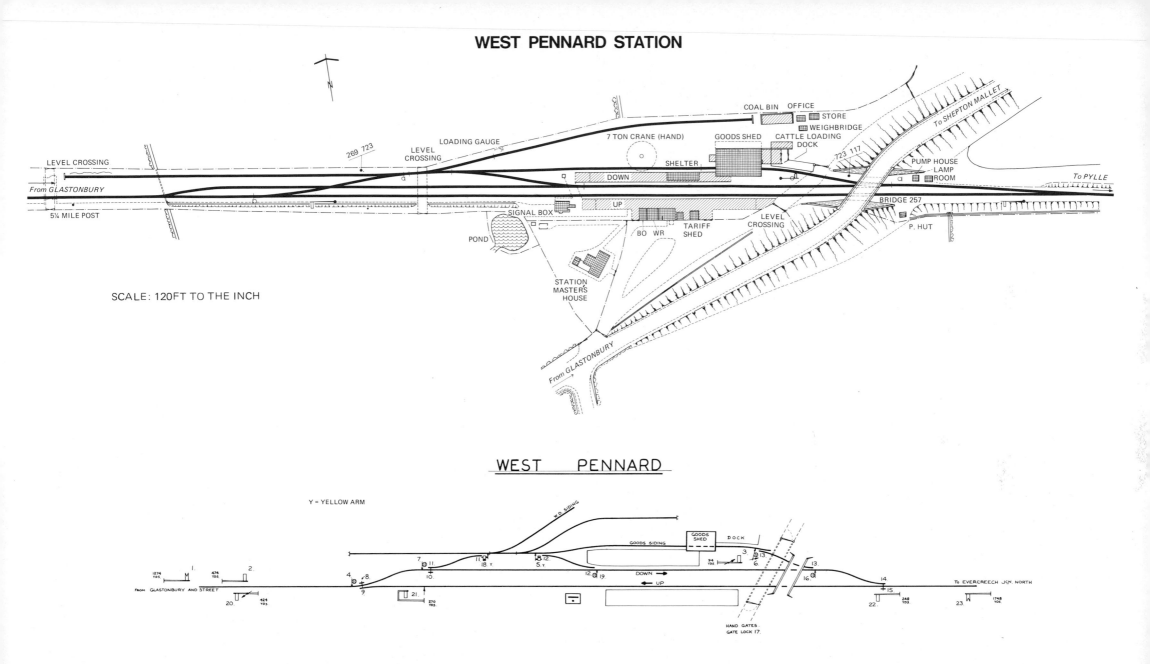

COAL BIN   OFFICE
STORE
WEIGHBRIDGE
LOADING GAUGE   7 TON CRANE (HAND)   GOODS SHED   CATTLE LOADING DOCK
269 723   LEVEL   SHELTER   723 117
                CROSSING   PUMP HOUSE
LEVEL CROSSING   DOWN   LAMP ROOM
From GLASTONBURY   To PYLLE
5¼ MILE POST   UP   BRIDGE 257
                          SIGNAL BOX   LEVEL   P. HUT
                      POND   BO WR   TARIFF   CROSSING
                                                      SHED
                                    STATION
                                    MASTERS
                                    HOUSE
From GLASTONBURY

To SHEPTON MALLET

SCALE: 120FT TO THE INCH

WEST   PENNARD

Y = YELLOW ARM

W.D. SIDING
GOODS
SHED   DOCK
GOODS SIDING
7 11   11   8 12   94   3
            18. Y   5. Y   YDS   13
4   8   12   19   6
                                                DOWN   13
1274   474   2.   10   16
YDS.   YDS.   14
From GLASTONBURY AND STREET   9   UP   15   To EVERCREECH JCN. NORTH
            20   424   21.   270   22   248   23   1748
                        YDS.   YDS.   YDS.   YDS.

HAND GATES
GATE LOCK 17.

99

West Pennard The up platform with the former tariff shed in the foreground. *Lens of Sutton*

West Pennard Not a busy day! *OPC collection*

West Pennard The signal box. *OPC collection*

West Pennard Note the siding entrance signal between the running lines; a view looking towards Glastonbury. *OPC collection*

Opened:	28 August 1854
Closed:	7 March 1966 (to all traffic)
Renaming:	'Glastonbury' until July 1886 when it first appeared in the timetables with the suffix '& Street'.
Plan date:	1920

Glastonbury possessed a most imposing looking station with large canopies covering about half the length of each platform. The down platform was an island, the Wells branch train, for which this station was the junction, using the northern face until closure of the branch on 29th October, 1951. An ornate footbridge connected the two platforms instead of the more usual foot crossing. The station buildings were of wood and the station once boasted a refreshment room but this closed in the 'thirties.

The layout was comprehensive and included a very commodious goods yard complete with two hand cranes, cattle docks and goods shed. As well as the branch line already mentioned there was an up siding serving a loading dock and a line served the various offices and workshops of the Engineer.

A twenty nine lever signal box of Midland appearance controlled the layout except for the level crossing at the east end, which was worked from a separate and adjacent gatekeeper's hut.

Glastonbury   An early scene.
Courtesy R. Atthill

Glastonbury   The headquarters' offices of the S & D in Glastonbury from 1861-1877.
D. Milton

Glastonbury   Looking towards Shapwick; Wells branch at right. Note the co-acting arm on the down starting signal.
OPC collection

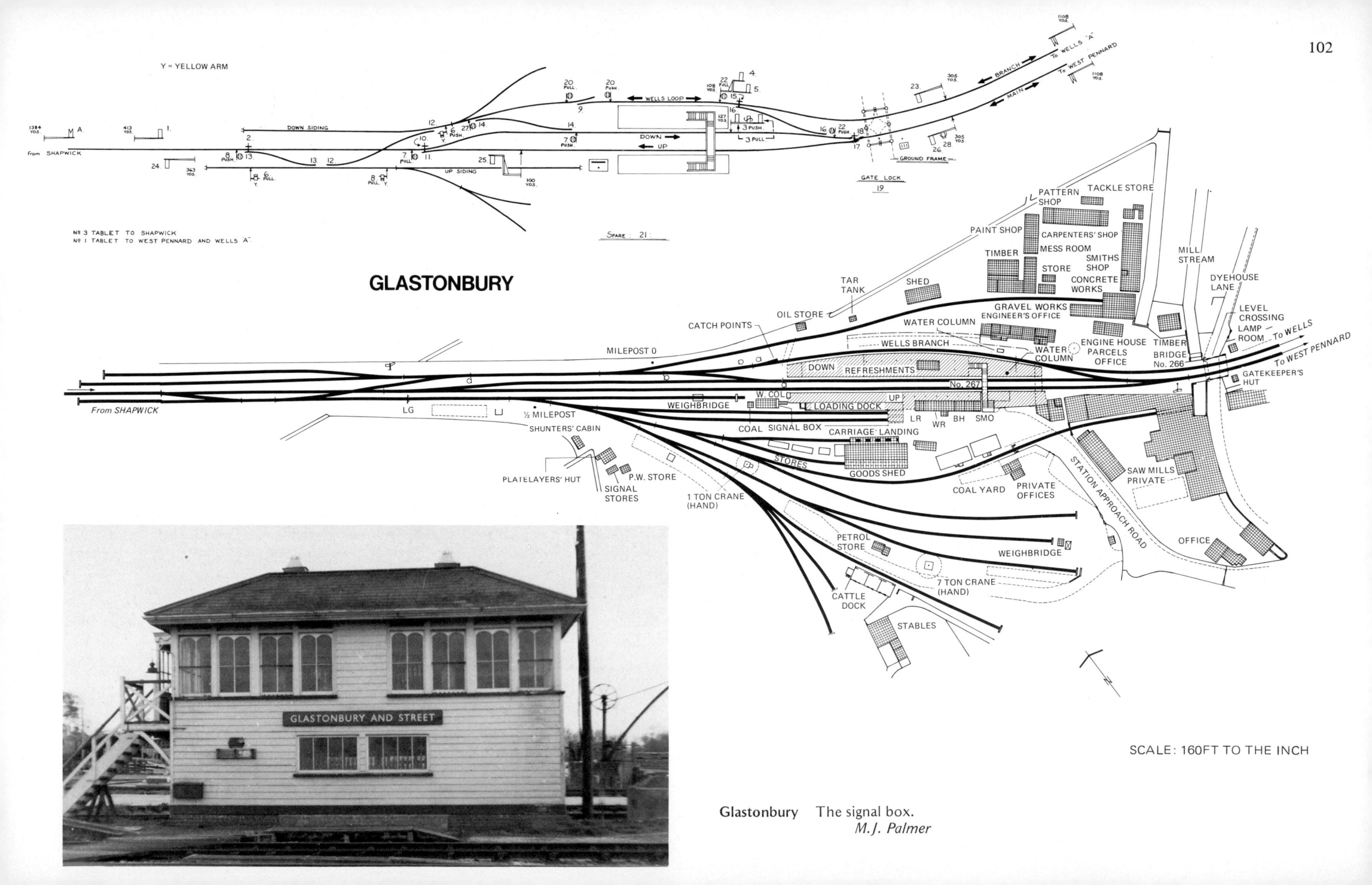

Y = YELLOW ARM

20 PULL
20 PUSH

WELLS LOOP

4.
22 PULL
108 YDS.
5.
15
22 PUSH
127 YDS.

1108 YDS.
To WELLS 'A'
To WEST PENNARD
BRANCH
MAIN
1108 YDS.

23
305 YDS.

9.

3 PUSH
3 PULL

DOWN SIDING

12
6
27
14

14

16
22 PUSH
18

17

305 YDS.
26
28

1384 YDS.
M A

413 YDS.
1.
2.

10

DOWN
7
PUSH

GROUND FRAME

From SHAPWICK

8 PUSH
13

8
Y

13 12

7
PULL
11

25

UP

GATE LOCK
19

24.

363 YDS.

6
PULL Y

8
PULL Y

UP SIDING

100 YDS.

Spare : 21

Nº 3 TABLET TO SHAPWICK
Nº 1 TABLET TO WEST PENNARD AND WELLS 'A'

GLASTONBURY

CATCH POINTS

TAR
TANK

SHED

PATTERN
SHOP

TACKLE STORE

PAINT SHOP

CARPENTERS' SHOP

MESS ROOM

TIMBER

STORE

SMITHS
SHOP

MILL
STREAM

DYEHOUSE
LANE

CONCRETE
WORKS

OIL STORE

GRAVEL WORKS
ENGINEER'S OFFICE

WATER COLUMN

LEVEL
CROSSING

MILEPOST 0

WELLS BRANCH

WATER
COLUMN

ENGINE HOUSE
PARCELS
OFFICE

TIMBER
BRIDGE
No. 266

LAMP
ROOM

To WELLS

DOWN
REFRESHMENTS

UP

No. 267

To WEST PENNARD

W. COL

GATEKEEPER'S
HUT

From SHAPWICK

LG

½ MILEPOST

WEIGHBRIDGE

LOADING DOCK

LR
WR

BH
SMO

SHUNTERS' CABIN

COAL SIGNAL BOX

CARRIAGE LANDING

STORES

GOODS SHED

SAW MILLS
PRIVATE

PLATELAYERS' HUT

SIGNAL
STORES

P.W. STORE

1 TON CRANE
(HAND)

COAL YARD

PRIVATE
OFFICES

STATION APPROACH ROAD

OFFICE

PETROL
STORE

WEIGHBRIDGE

7 TON CRANE
(HAND)

CATTLE
DOCK

STABLES

SCALE: 160FT TO THE INCH

Glastonbury   The signal box.
M.J. Palmer

GLASTONBURY AND STREET

Glastonbury Looking towards West Pennard. The Wells branch comes out from behind the island platform and is the left hand line approaching the crossing. *OPC collection*

Glastonbury This shows clearly the commodious canopies provided. *OPC collection*

Glastonbury A view towards Shapwick taken from the footbridge. Note Midland style signal box at left. *OPC collection*

Glastonbury Looking west. *M.J. Palmer*

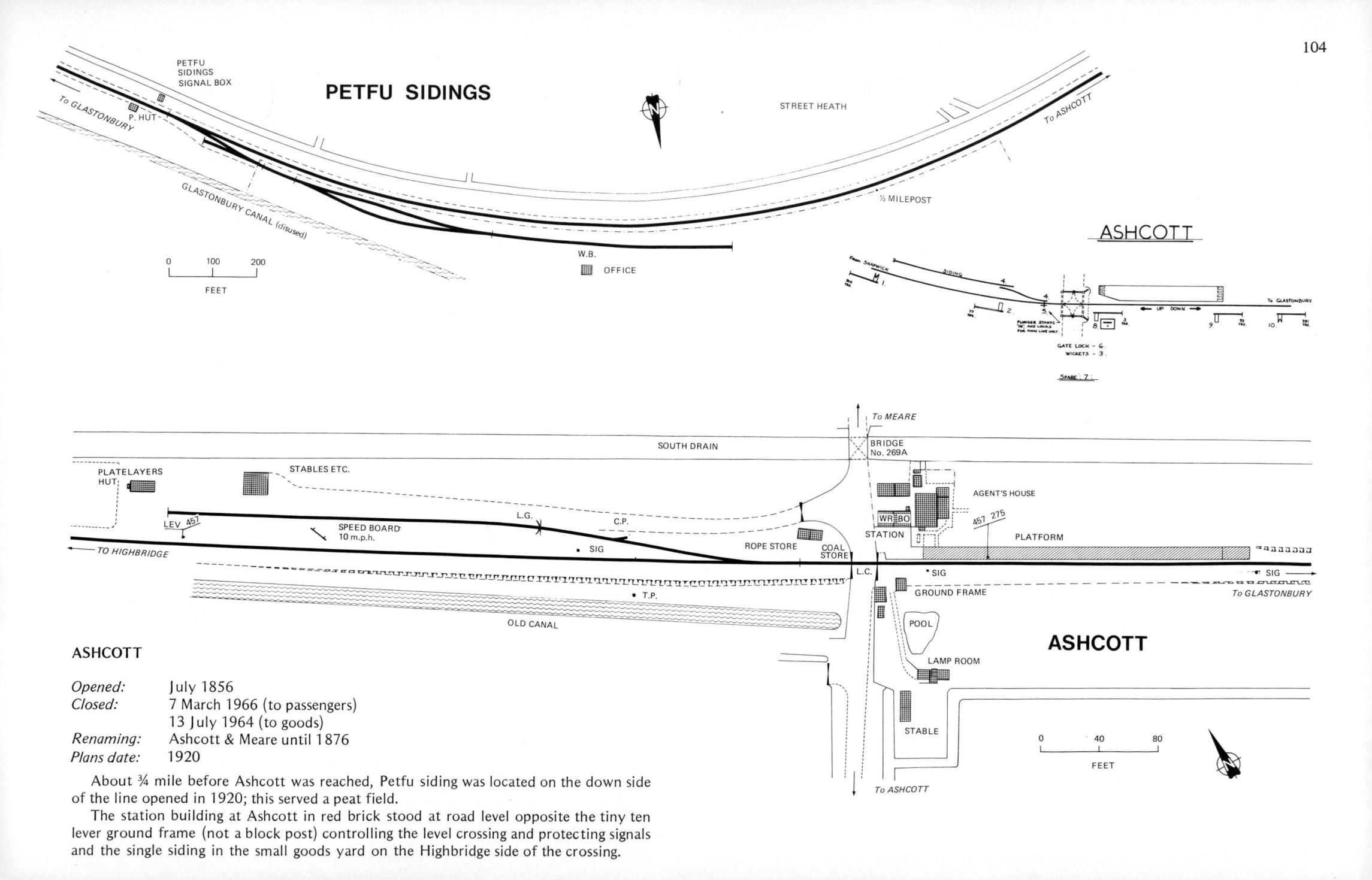

PETFU SIDINGS

PETFU
SIDINGS
SIGNAL BOX

To GLASTONBURY

P. HUT

GLASTONBURY CANAL (disused)

STREET HEATH

To ASHCOTT

½ MILEPOST

0   100   200

FEET

W.B.

OFFICE

ASHCOTT

From SHAPWICK
SIDING
To GLASTONBURY
UP   DOWN

PLUNGER STANDS
'IN', AND LOCKS
FOR MAIN LINE ONLY

GATE LOCK - 6.
WICKETS - 3.

SPARE : 7.

SOUTH DRAIN

To MEARE

BRIDGE
No. 269A

PLATELAYERS
HUT

STABLES ETC.

AGENT'S HOUSE

LEV 457

SPEED BOARD
10 m.p.h.

L.G.

C.P.

WR BO

457 275

STATION

PLATFORM

TO HIGHBRIDGE

ROPE STORE

COAL
STORE

SIG

L.C.

SIG

SIG

To GLASTONBURY

GROUND FRAME

T.P.

OLD CANAL

POOL

LAMP ROOM

ASHCOTT

STABLE

0   40   80

FEET

To ASHCOTT

ASHCOTT

Opened: July 1856
Closed: 7 March 1966 (to passengers)
13 July 1964 (to goods)
Renaming: Ashcott & Meare until 1876
Plans date: 1920

About ¾ mile before Ashcott was reached, Petfu siding was located on the down side of the line opened in 1920; this served a peat field.

The station building at Ashcott in red brick stood at road level opposite the tiny ten lever ground frame (not a block post) controlling the level crossing and protecting signals and the single siding in the small goods yard on the Highbridge side of the crossing.

Ashcott   Towards Shapwick.   *OPC Collection*

Ashcott   This view clearly shows the original wooden platform and rustic seats.
OPC Collection

Ashcott   The simple concrete platform photographed from the roadway. *Lens of Sutton*

Ashcott   The ground frame and crossing gates.   *OPC collection*

ALEXANDER'S SIDING

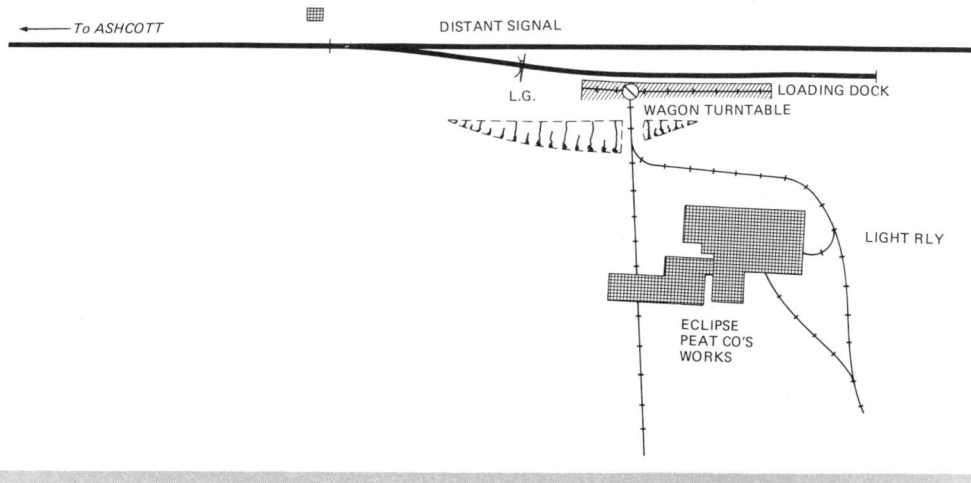

ALEXANDER'S SIDING LEVER BOX

To ASHCOTT

DISTANT SIGNAL

To SHAPWICK

L.G.   LOADING DOCK

WAGON TURNTABLE

LIGHT RLY

ECLIPSE
PEAT CO'S
WORKS

0   100   200

FEET

ALEXANDER'S SIDING

Plan date: 1920

Situated between Ashcott and Shapwick and some half a mile west of the former, Alexander's siding served the Eclipse Peat Company's works. A 2 ft tramway from the works to the nearby peat beds crossed the Somerset & Dorset on the level.

SHAPWICK

Opened:	28 August 1854
Closed:	7 March 1966 (to passengers)
	10 June 1963 (to goods)
Plan date:	1921

Shapwick was a block post with a long crossing loop and a couple of sidings on the up side. The station building was a fairly simple wooden structure on the up platform whilst nothing at all was provided on the down platform.

The signal box stood close by the level crossing and dated from the turn of the century when the station was rebuilt following a fire. Built completely of wood the box contained seventeen levers and remained in use until closure of the line.

A substantial traffic in peat was dealt with here until the major development of road transport in the years following the First World War.

Shapwick   The lattice post of the down inner home signal looks a trifle battered!

OPC collection

SHAPWICK

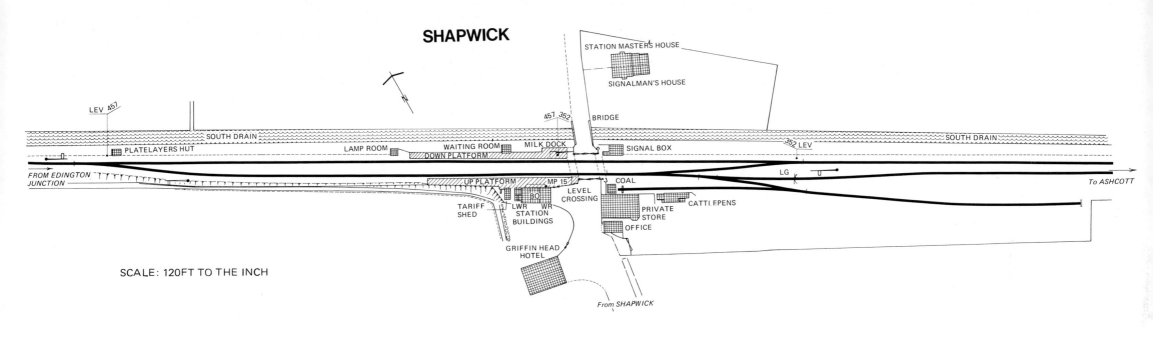

LEV 457

STATION MASTERS HOUSE

SIGNALMAN'S HOUSE

457 352   BRIDGE

SOUTH DRAIN   SOUTH DRAIN

PLATELAYERS HUT   LAMP ROOM   WAITING ROOM   MILK DOCK   SIGNAL BOX   352 LEV

DOWN PLATFORM

FROM EDINGTON   UP PLATFORM   MP 15   COAL   LG
JUNCTION   LEVEL   To ASHCOTT
CROSSING

TARIFF   LWR WR   PRIVATE   CATTLE PENS
SHED   STATION   STORE
BUILDINGS   OFFICE

GRIFFIN HEAD   From SHAPWICK
HOTEL

SCALE: 120FT TO THE INCH

SHAPWICK

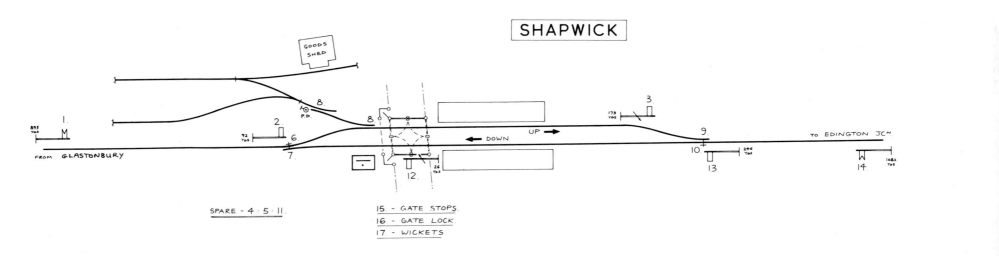

GOODS
SHED

8

1   8

2   8   8   3
173
YDS

892
YDS   92
YDS   DOWN   UP   9   To EDINGTON JCN

6   246
FROM GLASTONBURY   7   10   YDS
12   13   14
26   1082
YDS   YDS

SPARE - 4·5·11

15 - GATE STOPS
16 - GATE LOCK
17 - WICKETS

107

Shapwick The seventeen lever signal box.

OPC Collection

Shapwick The wooden building on the up platform.

OPC collection

Shapwick Towards Ashcott.

Lens of Sutton

Shapwick Towards Edington Jc.; note long crossing loop.

OPC collection

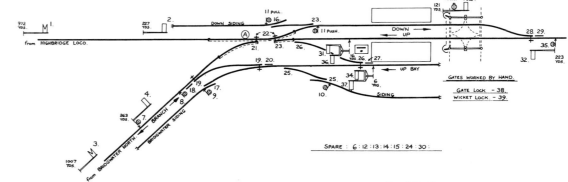

EDINGTON JUNCTION

Opened: 1856

Closed: 7 March 1966 (to passengers)
13 July 1964 (to goods)

Renaming: 'Edington Road' until 21 July 1890
'Edington Junction' until 8 June 1953
'Edington Burtle' thereafter

Plan date: 1921

Edington was the junction for the Bridgwater branch which had a short life, opening in 1890 and closing to passengers on 1st December, 1952. The layout at the junction was quite impressive and the platforms were well provided with buildings. The principal building stood at the southern end of the up platform and a wooden shelter and staff rooms were situated on the down platform. The station master's house stood on the down side of the line just short of the level crossing, the gates of which were remote from the signal box and worked by hand although locked in the box.

The Bridgwater branch closed completely in October 1954 and in February 1956 the down crossing loop, down platform and all sidings except that leading to the goods shed were taken out of use. At the same time the thirty nine lever signal box closed, the connection to the remaining siding being worked by a ground frame as was the locking for the crossing gates. In fact, the box, crossing loop and down platform had all been out of *regular* use since the withdrawal of the branch passenger service.

After the closure of the Bridgwater branch to passengers the station was renamed Edington Burtle.

EDINGTON JUNCTION

Edington Junction The station in 1959 after closure of the Bridgwater branch and removal of the loop.
OPC Collection

Edington Junction Looking towards Shapwick after being renamed Edington Burtle.
Lens of Sutton

BASON BRIDGE

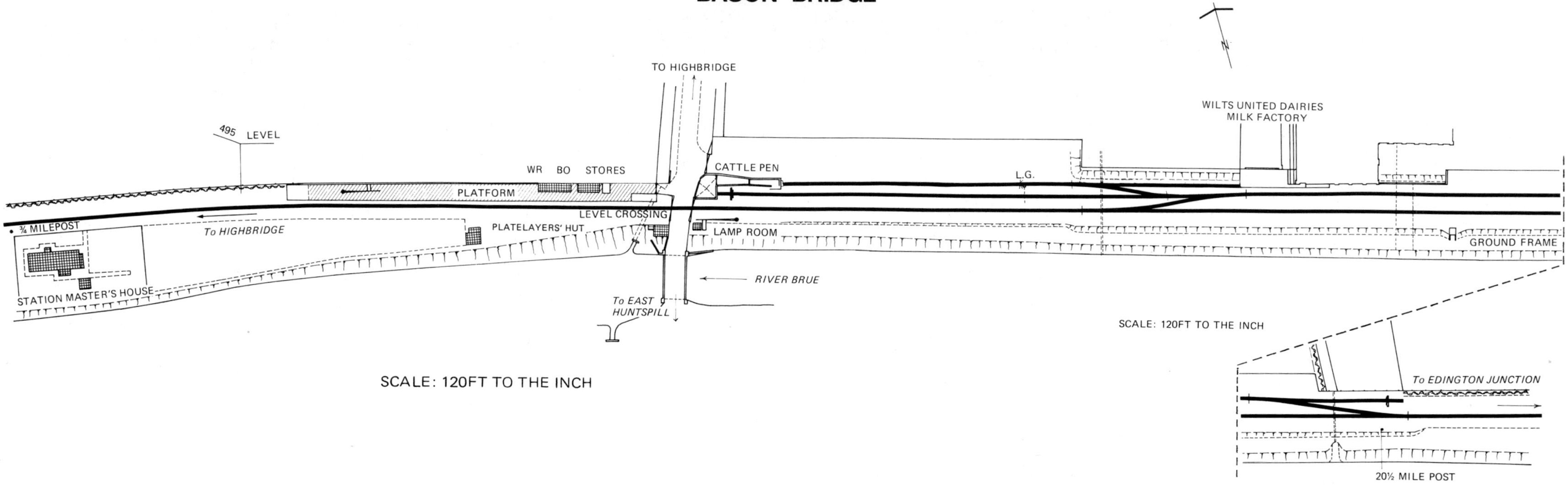

TO HIGHBRIDGE

WILTS UNITED DAIRIES
MILK FACTORY

495 LEVEL

WR BO STORES

CATTLE PEN

L.G.

PLATFORM

LEVEL CROSSING

¾ MILEPOST

To HIGHBRIDGE

PLATELAYERS' HUT

LAMP ROOM

GROUND FRAME

STATION MASTER'S HOUSE

RIVER BRUE

To EAST
HUNTSPILL

SCALE: 120FT TO THE INCH

SCALE: 120FT TO THE INCH

To EDINGTON JUNCTION

20½ MILE POST

BASON BRIDGE

Opened: July 1856
Closed: 7 March 1966 (to passengers)
               10 June 1963 (to public goods traffic)
               2 October 1972 (entirely — milk tanks only handled since withdrawal of
               passenger service)
               Milk factory (Wilts United Dairies) built in 1909.
Plan date: 1921

The principal activity at Bason Bridge was a milk factory owned by United Dairies which loaded milk tanks by rail to London. Because of this the section of line from Highbridge to Bason Bridge did not close until 2nd October, 1972 (when this rail flow of milk ceased — some years after the closure of the rest of the branch).

The sidings serving the factory were controlled from the East ground frame whilst the level crossing was worked from the West ground frame.

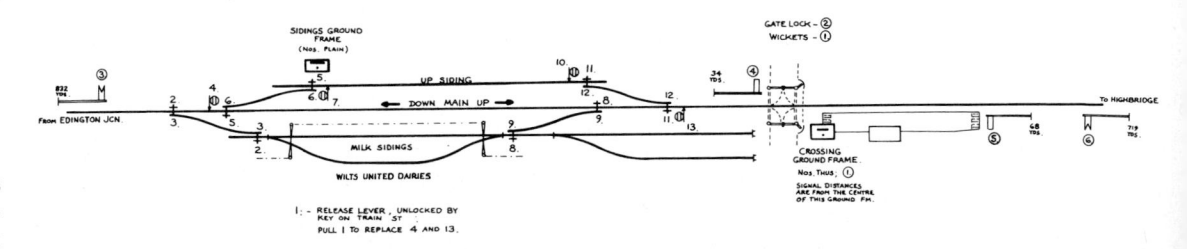

BASON BRIDGE

Bason Bridge   The neat wooden station buildings in 1960.   *D. Milton*

Bason Bridge   The view towards Highbridge with the station master's house in the distance.   *D. Milton*

Bason Bridge   As can be seen the platform was somewhat cramped.   *Lens of Sutton*

Bason Bridge   Looking east; August 1959.   *R.H. Clark*

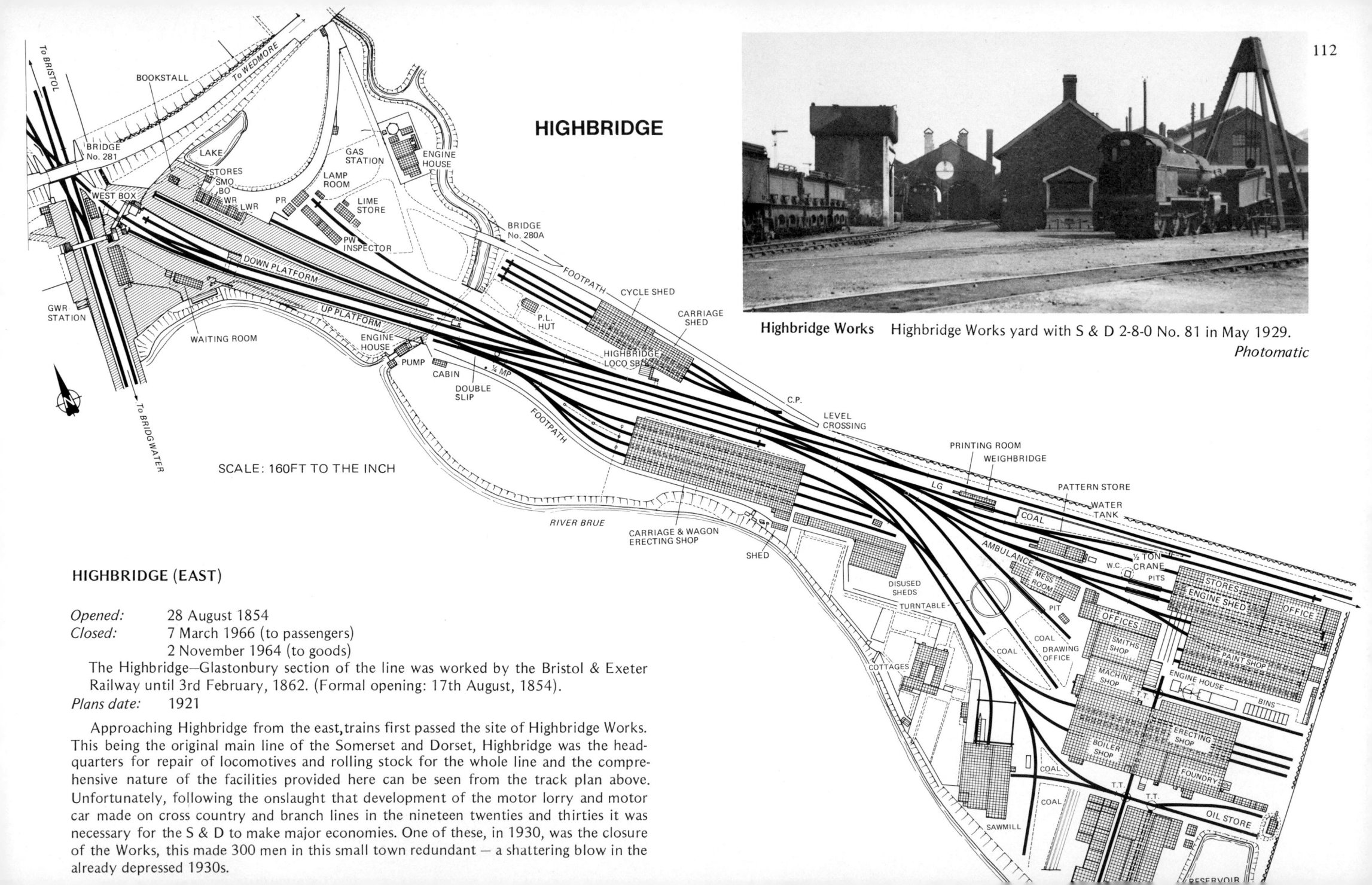

HIGHBRIDGE

Labels on track plan: To BRISTOL, To WEDMORE, BOOKSTALL, BRIDGE No. 281, LAKE, GAS STATION, ENGINE HOUSE, STORES, SMO, BO, WR, LWR, LAMP ROOM, LIME STORE, PR, PW INSPECTOR, WEST BOX, GWR STATION, DOWN PLATFORM, UP PLATFORM, WAITING ROOM, To BRIDGWATER, ENGINE HOUSE, PUMP, CABIN, DOUBLE SLIP, ¼ MP, FOOTPATH, BRIDGE No. 280A, P.L. HUT, CYCLE SHED, CARRIAGE SHED, HIGHBRIDGE LOCO SHED, C.P., LEVEL CROSSING, PRINTING ROOM, WEIGHBRIDGE, PATTERN STORE, WATER TANK, LG, COAL, RIVER BRUE, CARRIAGE & WAGON ERECTING SHOP, SHED, AMBULANCE, MESS ROOM, ½ TON CRANE, W.C., PITS, STORES, ENGINE SHED, OFFICE, DISUSED SHEDS, TURNTABLE, PIT, COAL, COAL DRAWING OFFICE, OFFICES, SMITHS SHOP, PAINT SHOP, ENGINE HOUSE, COTTAGES, MACHINE SHOP, T.T., BINS, BOILER SHOP, ERECTING SHOP, FOUNDRY, COAL, T.T., OIL STORE, SAWMILL, RESERVOIR

SCALE: 160FT TO THE INCH

Highbridge Works Highbridge Works yard with S & D 2-8-0 No. 81 in May 1929.
Photomatic

HIGHBRIDGE (EAST)

Opened: 28 August 1854
Closed: 7 March 1966 (to passengers)
                2 November 1964 (to goods)
The Highbridge—Glastonbury section of the line was worked by the Bristol & Exeter Railway until 3rd February, 1862. (Formal opening: 17th August, 1854).
Plans date: 1921

Approaching Highbridge from the east, trains first passed the site of Highbridge Works. This being the original main line of the Somerset and Dorset, Highbridge was the headquarters for repair of locomotives and rolling stock for the whole line and the comprehensive nature of the facilities provided here can be seen from the track plan above. Unfortunately, following the onslaught that development of the motor lorry and motor car made on cross country and branch lines in the nineteen twenties and thirties it was necessary for the S & D to make major economies. One of these, in 1930, was the closure of the Works, this made 300 men in this small town redundant — a shattering blow in the already depressed 1930s.

After the Works came Highbridge Loco Box. This twenty five lever box, apart from controlling the access to and egress from the Works layout, as its name would suggest, admitted engines to the two road engine shed and associated facilities. It also controlled the southern end of the station; surprisingly the bay platforms were signalled only for departing trains.

The S & D station at Highbridge had five platforms although two of the dead-end platforms only served one line. The principal building was situated at the buffer stops end of the terminal platforms and was of brick with stone facings. On the end wall nearest the Great Western line was a memorial in bronze commemorating the railwaymen of Highbridge who had served in the 1914-18 war. In its latter years having been relegated to the status of a branch and lost most of its traffic to road, Highbridge was something of a ghost station, particularly after closure of the line to Burnham to regular passenger trains in 1951.

At the northern end of the through platforms and just short of the flat crossing over the GWR stood 'A' box (closed in 1914) at which time control of the flat crossing was put entirely in the hands of Highbridge West (GWR) box. The signalling between the GWR box and Highbridge Loco was absolute block (double line) and the 100 yards or so of single line from the GWR box to Highbridge 'B' was single line block without a token.

Highbridge 'B' was a small box of twelve levers which controlled a level crossing and the access to the goods yard at Highbridge. Following closure of the Highbridge Wharf—Highbridge (GW) crossing section of line in 1965 a direct connection between the S & D (northern end of the through platforms) and the ex-GW goods yard was put in, by slewing the former Burnham single line into the ex-GW sidings.

Another short section of just over 300 yards brought trains to Highbridge 'C' Box — the single line section also being worked without a token. This was a nineteen lever box which, apart from controlling a busy level crossing (the A38), worked the junction between the single line to Burnham (operated by train staff and ticket) and the Highbridge Wharf sidings.

Following nationalisation the signal boxes were renamed as follows: Loco box became Highbridge East 'C', 'B' box became East 'B' and 'C' box became East 'A'. Highbridge East 'A' and East 'B' boxes both closed on 16th May, 1965 with the closure of the Highbridge wharves.

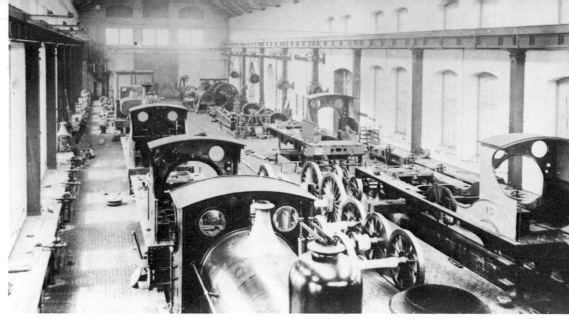

Highbridge Works   Inside the locomotive works about 1895.   *OPC collection*

Highbridge Works c.1900.   *R. Atthill collection*

Highbridge Works   After closure, September 1936.   *Photomatic*

Highbridge Shed   Coaling a 2-6-2T in April 1959.   *Photomatic*

Highbridge   Highbridge East 'C' box, January 1966.   *H.B. Oliver courtesy R. Atthill*

HIGHBRIDGE EAST 'C'

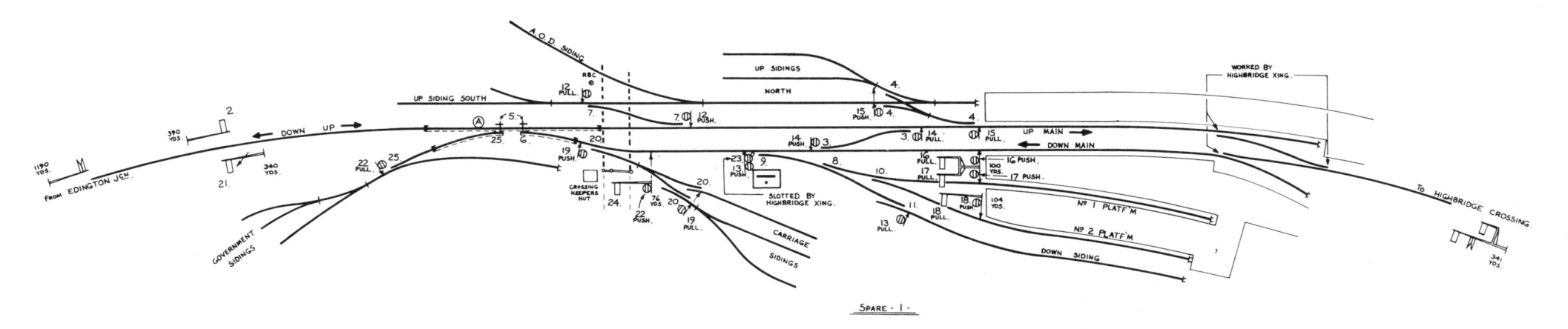

Highbridge   Looking towards Burnham from the platform ends.   *OPC collection*

Highbridge   A photograph taken from the Burnham end of the through platforms; old Highbridge 'A' box at right (closed 1914).   *OPC collection*

Highbridge   The Somerset & Dorset station c. 1910 with trains at the up platform and in the bay. The carriage and wagon erecting shop is in the distance.   *Lens of Sutton*

Highbridge   The well-known wedge-shaped GWR box (Highbridge West) in 1971. The Burnham line passed in front of the box and crossed the GWR on the level under the bridge.   *S. Devon Railway Museum*

Highbridge Looking towards Highbridge East 'C' (old 'Loco') box with Works at right.
OPC collection

Highbridge The connection from the GWR Taunton–Bristol line to the Burnham branch can be seen at far left.
OPC Collection

HIGHBRIDGE EAST 'B'

Highbridge Highbridge East 'B' box can be seen adjacent to level crossing in the background. GWR box at left.
OPC collection

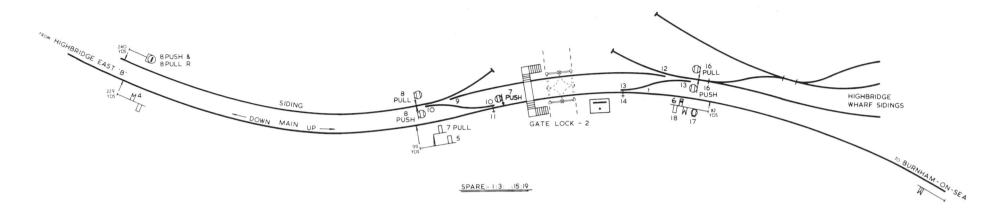

SPARE:- 1:3: :15:19

Highbridge   Highbridge 'C' in April 1932 . . . .   *R. Atthill*

Highbridge   . . . .and as it was following renaming Highbridge East 'A' in BR days.
D. Milton

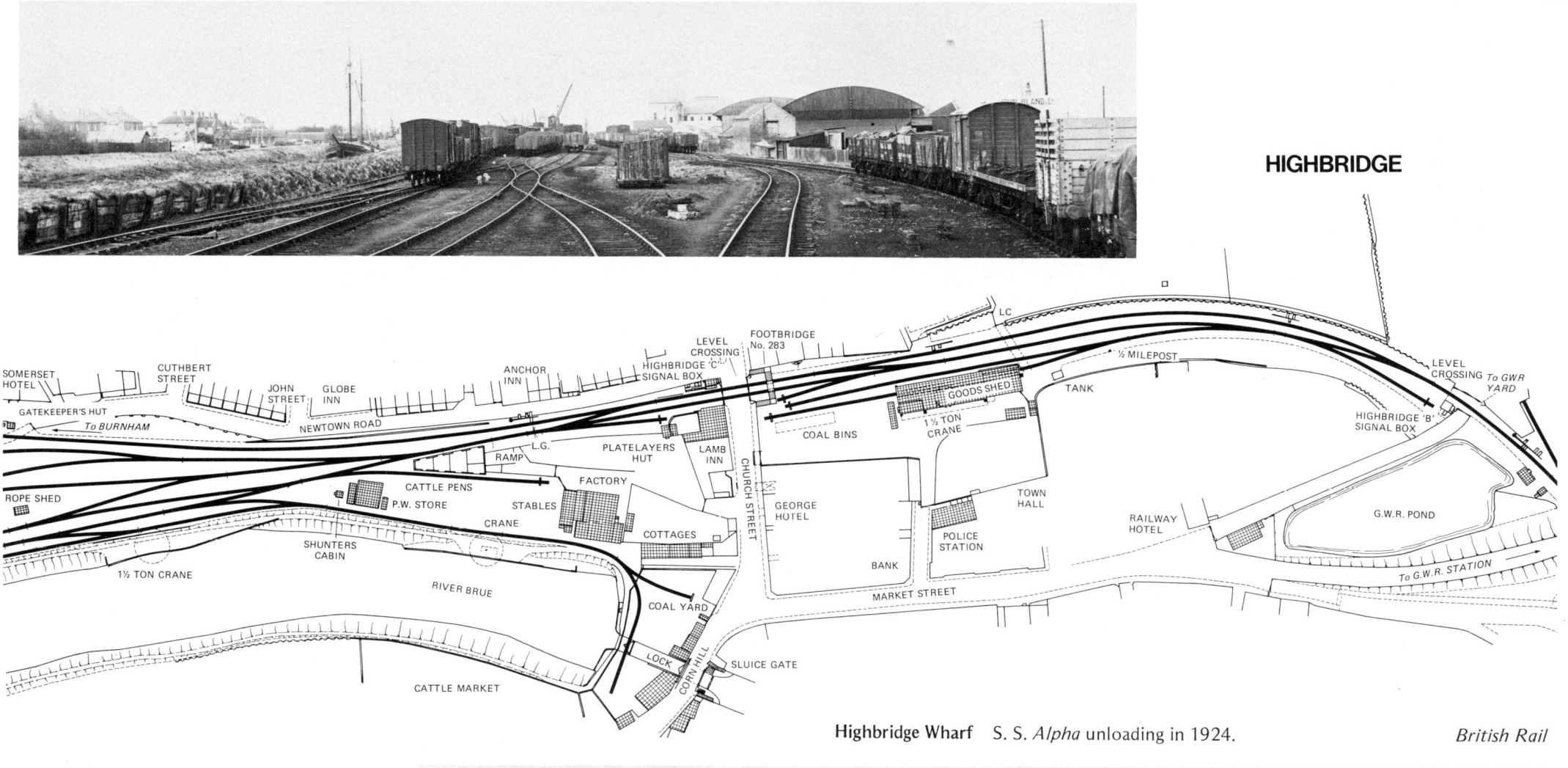

HIGHBRIDGE

SOMERSET HOTEL

CUTHBERT STREET

GATEKEEPER'S HUT

To BURNHAM

JOHN STREET

GLOBE INN

NEWTOWN ROAD

ANCHOR INN

LEVEL CROSSING

HIGHBRIDGE 'C' SIGNAL BOX

FOOTBRIDGE No. 283

LC

½ MILEPOST

LEVEL CROSSING

To GWR YARD

HIGHBRIDGE 'B' SIGNAL BOX

GOODS SHED

TANK

1 ½ TON CRANE

COAL BINS

L.G.

RAMP

PLATELAYERS HUT

LAMB INN

CHURCH STREET

ROPE SHED

CATTLE PENS

P.W. STORE

FACTORY

STABLES

CRANE

COTTAGES

GEORGE HOTEL

TOWN HALL

POLICE STATION

RAILWAY HOTEL

G.W.R. POND

BANK

To G.W.R. STATION

SHUNTERS CABIN

1 ½ TON CRANE

RIVER BRUE

COAL YARD

MARKET STREET

LOCK

CORN HILL

SLUICE GATE

CATTLE MARKET

SCALE: 160FT TO THE INCH

Highbridge Wharf S. S. *Alpha* unloading in 1924.   *British Rail*

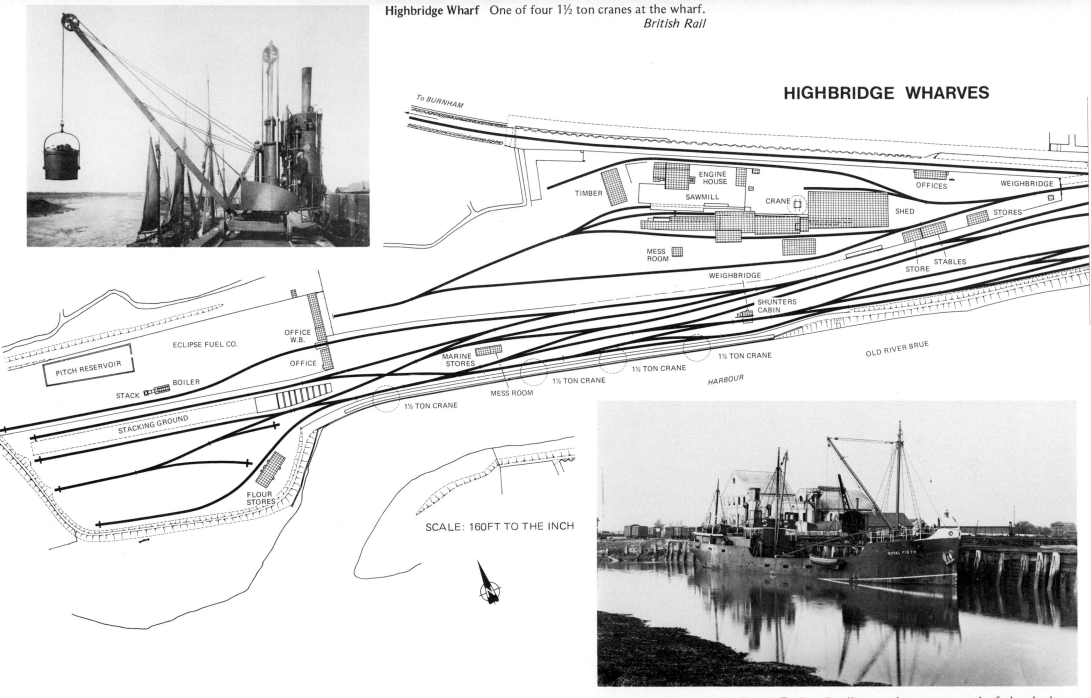

Highbridge Wharf One of four 1½ ton cranes at the wharf.
British Rail

HIGHBRIDGE WHARVES

To BURNHAM

TIMBER

ENGINE HOUSE

SAWMILL

CRANE

OFFICES

WEIGHBRIDGE

SHED

STORES

MESS ROOM

WEIGHBRIDGE

STABLES

STORE

SHUNTERS CABIN

ECLIPSE FUEL CO.

OFFICE W.B.

OFFICE

PITCH RESERVOIR

STACK   BOILER

MARINE STORES

MESS ROOM

1½ TON CRANE

1½ TON CRANE

1½ TON CRANE

OLD RIVER BRUE

HARBOUR

1½ TON CRANE

STACKING GROUND

FLOUR STORES

SCALE: 160FT TO THE INCH

Highbridge Wharf S. S. *Royal Firth* unloading at the western end of the docks.
British Rail

Burnham-on-Sea   Looking towards the sea.   *R. Atthill*

BURNHAM-ON-SEA

Opened:	3 May 1858
Closed:	29 October 1951 (to passengers except summer excursions)
	20 May 1963 (to goods)
Renaming:	'Burnham' until 12 July 1920
Plans dates:	1921 c. 1950's

The 1¾ mile extension from Highbridge to Burnham-on-Sea was opened in 1858. The short through platform (the line originally continued to Burnham pier although it is not thought passenger trains traversed the short section) was partly covered by a gloomy all-over roof which contained the station facilities. A tiny four lever signal box stood at the eastern end of the platform; this closed pre-1960. A red brick goods shed and limited freight facilities stood north of the passenger platform.

Some ¾ mile east of the station a ground frame released by the train staff gave access to the 'Apex' and 'Colthurst, Symons' sidings.

It is interesting to note that the rails on the jetty were also used for launching the lifeboat which was housed at the end of a short private siding adjacent to the west end of the station! However this ceased in the early years of this century.

A concrete built 'excursion' platform was added to the south of the main platforms, access to which was controlled at the eastern end by a ground frame. After closure of Burnham-on-Sea to regular passenger trains on 29th October, 1951 it continued to be used for excursion trains in the summer months until 8th September, 1962. Finally Burnham was closed completely, having remained open for goods, on 20th May, 1963.

Burnham-on-Sea   An aerial view showing the station at left with disused jetty beyond.
Aerofilms

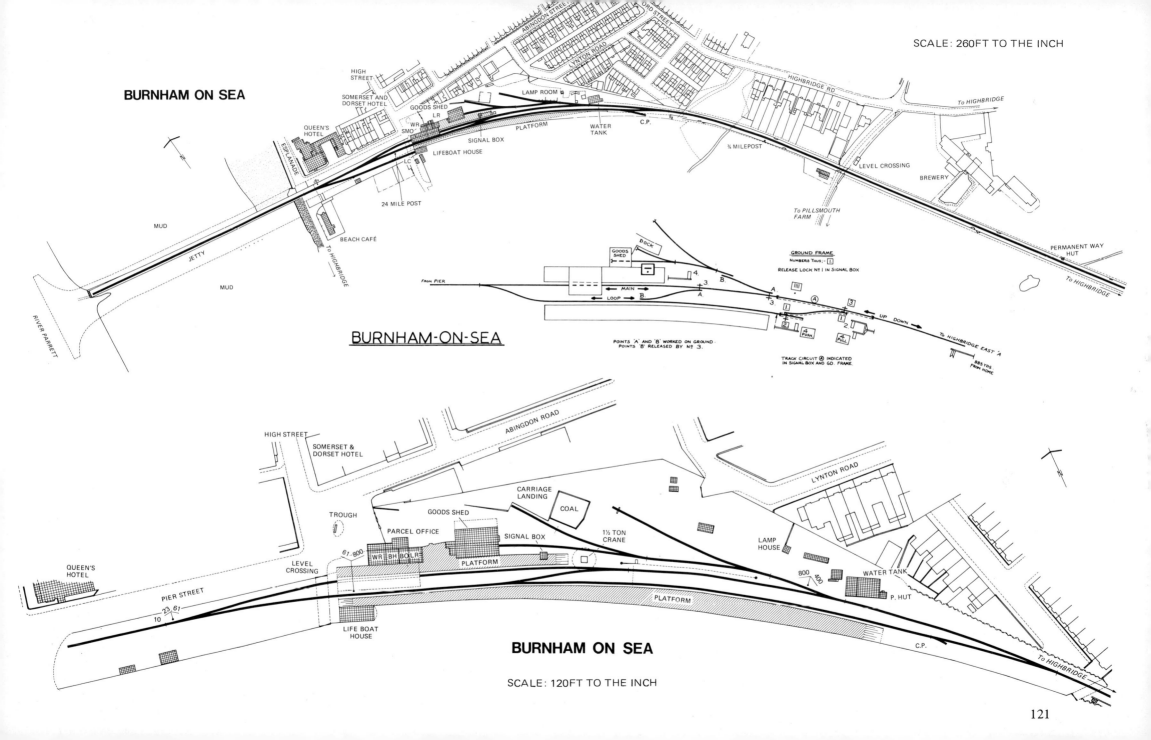

SCALE: 260FT TO THE INCH

BURNHAM ON SEA

To HIGHBRIDGE

HIGH STREET

SOMERSET AND DORSET HOTEL

LAMP ROOM

GOODS SHED

WR

SMO

LR

QUEEN'S HOTEL

ESPLANADE

SIGNAL BOX

LIFEBOAT HOUSE

LC

PLATFORM

WATER TANK

C.P.

¾ MILEPOST

LEVEL CROSSING

To PILLSMOUTH FARM

BREWERY

24 MILE POST

MUD

JETTY

To HIGHBRIDGE

BEACH CAFÉ

MUD

RIVER PARRETT

PERMANENT WAY HUT

To HIGHBRIDGE

BURNHAM-ON-SEA

FROM PIER

GOODS SHED

DOCK

MAIN

LOOP

B.

A.

3

B.

A

4

3

A

3

GROUND FRAME

NUMBERS THUS:- [1]

RELEASE LOCK No 1 IN SIGNAL BOX

(A)

1

3

2

4 PUSH

1

4 PULL

UP DOWN

To HIGHBRIDGE EAST 'A'

POINTS 'A' AND 'B' WORKED ON GROUND.
POINTS 'B' RELEASED BY No 3.

TRACK CIRCUIT (A) INDICATED
IN SIGNAL BOX AND GD. FRAME.

885 YDS.
FROM HOME

BURNHAM ON SEA

HIGH STREET

SOMERSET & DORSET HOTEL

ABINGDON ROAD

LYNTON ROAD

TROUGH

CARRIAGE LANDING

COAL

PARCEL OFFICE

GOODS SHED

SIGNAL BOX

1½ TON CRANE

LAMP HOUSE

QUEEN'S HOTEL

LEVEL CROSSING

61-800

WR BH BO LR

PLATFORM

800

400

WATER TANK

PIER STREET

10 23 61

LIFE BOAT HOUSE

PLATFORM

P. HUT

C.P.

To HIGHBRIDGE

SCALE: 120FT TO THE INCH

121

Burnham-on-Sea   The signal box in 1961.

R. Atthill

Burnham-on-Sea   The gloomy station building with overall roof.   *OPC collection*

Burnham-on-Sea   The truly gloomy interior; note signal box at the platform end.
OPC collection

Burnham-on-Sea   The stone work supporting the overall roof gives the building more of the look of a goods shed than a passenger station.   *OPC collection*

The Wells Branch

POLSHAM

Opened: December 1861
Closed: 29 October 1951 (passenger and goods)
Plan date: 1922

Facilities here were extremely simple consisting of a 200 feet long platform and single siding worked from a ground frame which also controlled the level crossing. The halt was closed on 29th October, 1951.

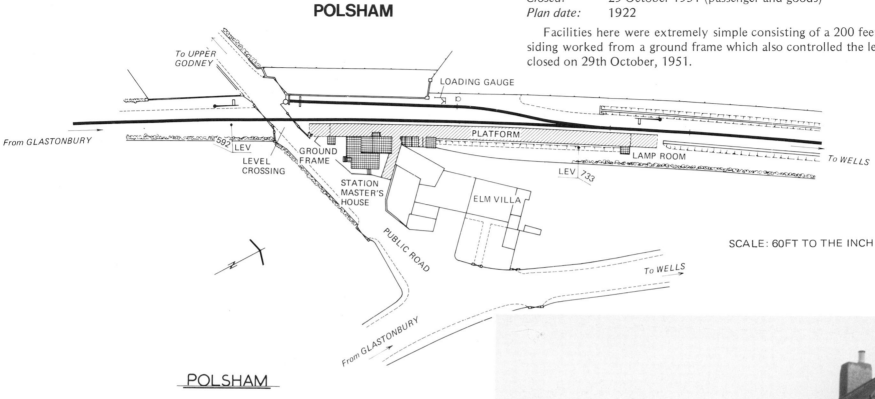

To UPPER GODNEY

LOADING GAUGE

From GLASTONBURY

592 LEV

LEVEL CROSSING

GROUND FRAME

STATION MASTER'S HOUSE

ELM VILLA

PUBLIC ROAD

PLATFORM

LAMP ROOM

LEV 733

To WELLS

To WELLS

From GLASTONBURY

SCALE: 60FT TO THE INCH

POLSHAM

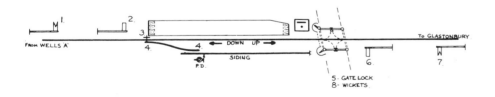

FROM WELLS 'A'

DOWN   UP

SIDING

P.D.

To GLASTONBURY

5 - GATE LOCK
8 - WICKETS

Polsham   From the south; station master's house at right.   *M. O'Connor*

WELLS (PRIORY ROAD)

Opened: 15 March 1859
Closed: 29 October 1951 (to passengers)
13 July 1964 (to goods)
Renamings: 'Wells' until October 1883 (passenger station)
'Wells' until 26 September 1949 (goods depot)
Plan date: 1922

Although a Cathedral City, Wells certainly did not justify the three stations it at one time possessed. These arose from the complicated nature of its railway history. The Somerset Central was first on the scene with its branch from Glastonbury opening on 15th March, 1859; its station was known as Wells Priory Road. Next came the East Somerset Railway from Witham opened on 1st March, 1862; its station was Wells East Somerset, south of Priory Road. Finally, the Cheddar Valley & Yatton Railway entered Wells from the north arriving at its Tucker St.station on 5th April, 1870. The other two railways in Wells were broad gauge whilst of course the S & D was narrow gauge. It was not until 1874/5 that the two broad gauge lines were made standard gauge,and not until 1st January, 1878 did passenger trains run through from the Cheddar Company to the East Somerset Company (both lines having now been absorbed by the GWR), over the intervening nine chains of S & D property.

Because of this historical background although GWR trains from Yatton to Witham ran past the S & D station at Wells they did not call for 56 years. The GWR station became Tucker Street; the East Somerset station was relegated to a goods station. It was not until 1934 that the ex S & D station at Priory Road was jointly used and then only until its early closure on 29th October, 1951.

Entering Wells from the Glastonbury direction S & D trains first passed the two road engine shed on the up side of the line. This was removed in December 1955. Next came the attractive signal box located just west of the junction with the GWR. Goods trains crossed this junction on the flat to gain access to the well laid out goods facilities including a large stone built goods shed. Passenger trains took the right hand curve to the GWR and ended their journey in the small through station with its overall roof and fine stone building. The branch train would be shunted into the adjacent lay-by siding to release the single line for GWR trains until the time for its return.

Wells S & D station closed together with its branch to Glastonbury on 29th October, 1951 but the goods depot continued to be served by GW trains. After closure of the S & D branch a short portion was retained to give access to the goods yard. The frame at East Somerset was altered to provide control over the remaining points and signals.

Wells The goods shed is on the left and Priory Rd passenger station on the right. The GWR line enters from the left of the picture. *OPC collection*

Wells The neat and attractive station buildings at Priory Road. *OPC Collection*

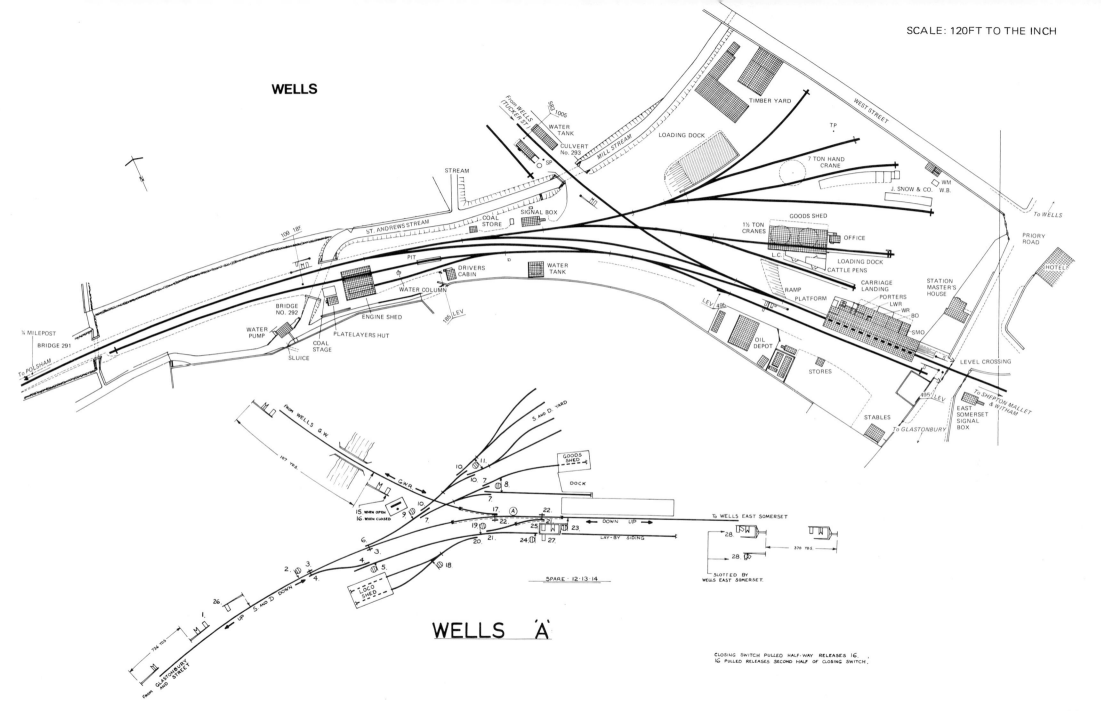

SCALE: 120FT TO THE INCH

WELLS

From WELLS (TUCKER ST.)

563 1005

WATER TANK

CULVERT No. 293

MILL STREAM

LOADING DOCK

TIMBER YARD

WEST STREET

SP

TP

7 TON HAND CRANE

To WELLS

STREAM

ST. ANDREWS STREAM

COAL STORE

SIGNAL BOX

J. SNOW & CO.

WM W.B.

GOODS SHED

1½ TON CRANES

OFFICE

PRIORY ROAD

HOTEL

109 18F

PIT

DRIVERS CABIN

WATER TANK

D

L.C.

LOADING DOCK

CATTLE PENS

STATION MASTER'S HOUSE

WATER COLUMN

RAMP

PLATFORM

CARRIAGE LANDING

PORTERS

LWR

WR

BO

¼ MILEPOST

BRIDGE No. 292

ENGINE SHED

185 LEV

LEV 495

SMO

BRIDGE 291

WATER PUMP

COAL STAGE

PLATELAYERS HUT

WATER TANK

OIL DEPOT

LEVEL CROSSING

To POLSHAM

SLUICE

STORES

STABLES

495 LEV

To SHEPTON MALLET & WITHAM

EAST SOMERSET SIGNAL BOX

To GLASTONBURY

FROM WELLS G.W.

5 AND D. YARD

GOODS SHED

DOCK

To WELLS EAST SOMERSET

107 YDS.

GWR

10 11

10

10. 7

8.

7.

17

(A)

22.

DOWN UP

28.

370 YDS.

15 WHEN OPEN
16 WHEN CLOSED

9

10

7

19

22

25 21 23

LAY-BY SIDING

28.

SLOTTED BY WELLS EAST SOMERSET.

6.

20. 21

24 27

3.

4.

5.

18

SPARE · 12·13·14

2. 3.

4

26

1.

UP S. AND D. DOWN

LOCO SHED

WELLS 'A'

736 YDS.

FROM GLASTONBURY AND STREET

CLOSING SWITCH PULLED HALF-WAY RELEASES 16.
16 PULLED RELEASES SECOND HALF OF CLOSING SWITCH.

Wells   A train approaches Priory Road from Wells Tucker St (ex-GWR).   *OPC collection*

Wells   Looking towards the junction with the GWR. The S & D signal box is switched out and the home signals for the GW line have been lowered in each direction. *OPC collection*

Wells   The East Somerset ex-GWR box.   *OPC collection*

Wells   A view towards the East Somerset (ex GWR) goods station; goods station towards the left, line to Shepton Mallet straight ahead and loco shed on right.   *OPC collection*

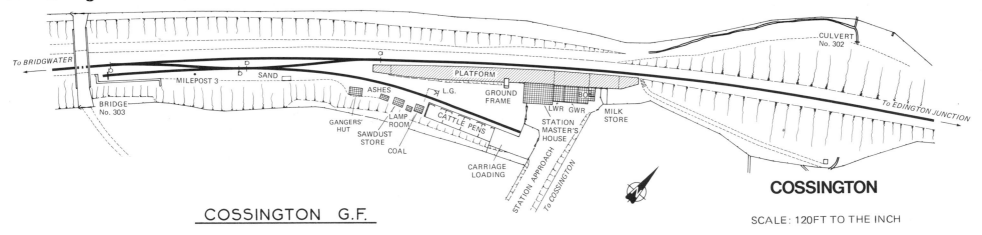

PLATFORM

GROUND FRAME

COSSINGTON

SCALE: 120FT TO THE INCH

COSSINGTON G.F.

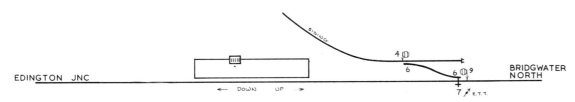

SPARES: 1.2.3 PUSH. 3 PULL. 5.8.10.

COSSINGTC

Opened: 21 July 1890
Closed: 1 December 1952 (to passengers)
4 October 1954 (to goods)
Plan date: 1923

Between Edington Junction and Cossington on the up side of the line was Board's siding which served a large quarry.

Cossington had a platform on the up side of the single line; station facilities consisted of a stone building adjacent to the station master's house. A ground frame worked the connection to the single siding which served cattle pens and an end loading dock.

The Bridgwater (sic) Railway Act of 1882 stipulated that at Cossington 'the Company shall construct and for ever hereafter maintain . . . a fit and suitable stone or brick building with convenient approaches and proper goods sidings'. However, when the British Transport Commission proposed closure in 1952 there were no legal objections. The station closed to passengers on 1st December, 1952.

Cossington The substantial stone buildings in 1960. *OPC Collection*

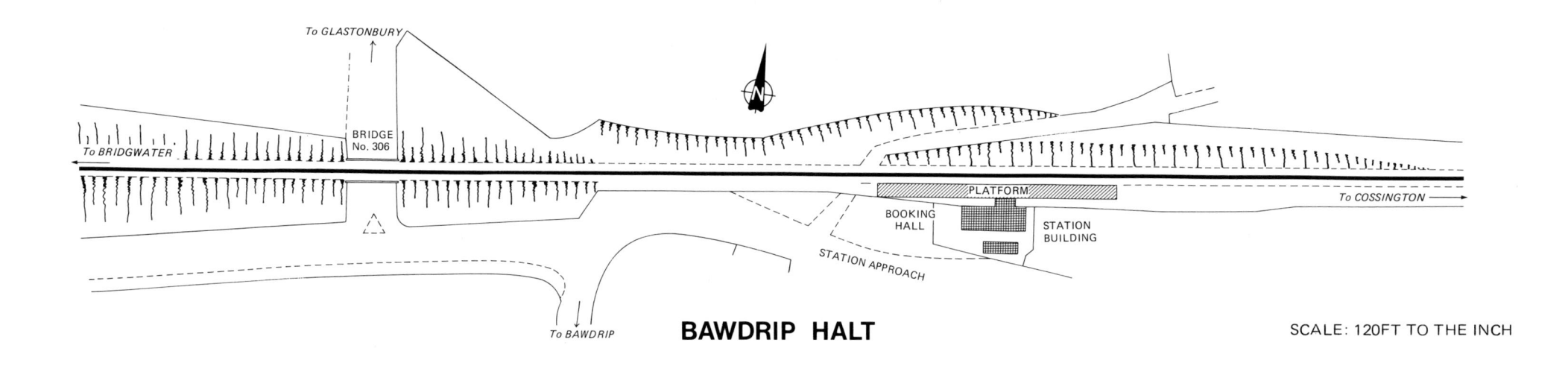

To GLASTONBURY

To BRIDGWATER

BRIDGE No. 306

N

PLATFORM

BOOKING HALL

STATION BUILDING

STATION APPROACH

To BAWDRIP

To COSSINGTON →

BAWDRIP HALT

SCALE: 120FT TO THE INCH

BAWDRIP HALT

Opened: 1923
Closed: 1 December 1952
Plan date: 1923

Just over a mile beyond Cossington stood Bawdrip Halt conveniently situated close to its village; the halt, built of concrete, opened in 1923 and closed on 1st December, 1952.

Bawdrip   A photograph taken not long after opening.

Bridgwater North   Gateway to Bournemouth!   *OPC collection*

Bridgwater North   A branch train waits in the departure platform.   *OPC collection*

Bridgwater North   The station building facing the roadway.   *OPC collection*

BRIDGWATER NORTH

Opened: 21 July 1890
Closed: 1 December 1952 (to passengers)
               4 October 1954 (to goods, but see below)
Plan date: 1923

Although the Bridgwater branch was always considered part of the S & D system it was built by an independent company, the Bridgwater Railway and opened on 21st July, 1890. However it was leased by the Somerset and Dorset from its inception until its nominal independence ended in 1923.

Just north of Bridgwater station a ground frame gave access to Board's siding serving a brick and tile works.

The brick built station building was quite handsome and was located at the buffer stops end of the island platform facing the town. The island platform was covered by an awning for more than half its length. A large goods yard was provided together with a brick built goods shed. A single road engine shed and 50 feet turntable were provided west of the goods yard.

A short branch line just over half a mile in length diverged from the goods yard sidings and ran to the bank of the River Parrett where it serviced wharves. These wharfages ceased to be used from the First World War and the track was removed during the Second World War for its scrap value.

Following complete closure of the branch in October 1954 a new connection was put in from the ex-GWR Docks branch to serve the goods yard at Bridgwater North. However this yard was out of use by the date of closure of the S & D system, 7th March, 1966.

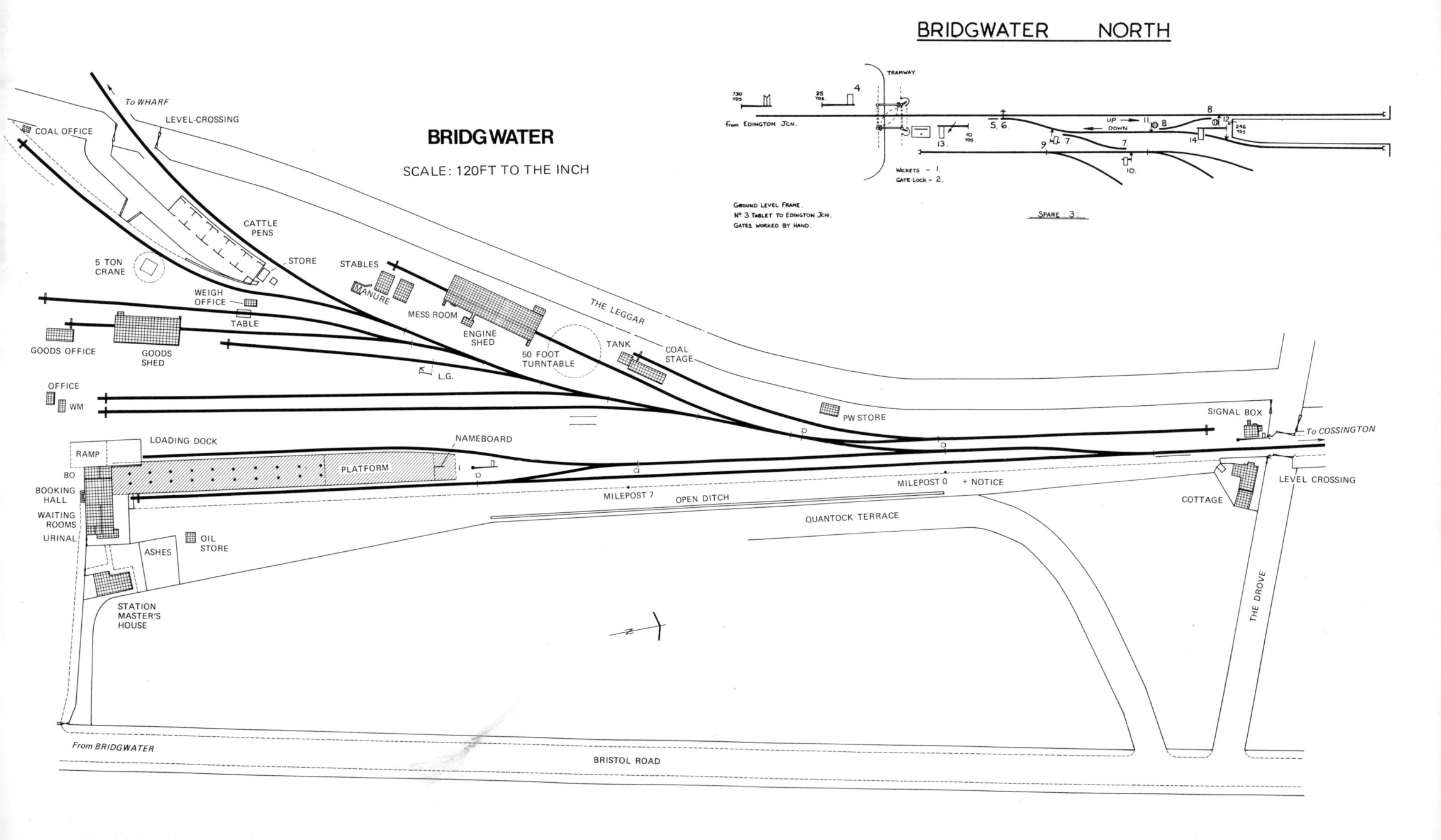

BRIDGWATER NORTH

BRIDGWATER

SCALE: 120FT TO THE INCH

To WHARF
LEVEL-CROSSING
COAL OFFICE
CATTLE PENS
STORE
STABLES
MANURE
5 TON CRANE
WEIGH OFFICE
TABLE
MESS ROOM
ENGINE SHED
50 FOOT TURNTABLE
THE LEGGAR
TANK
COAL STAGE
GOODS OFFICE
GOODS SHED
L.G.
OFFICE
WM
PW STORE
SIGNAL BOX
To COSSINGTON
LOADING DOCK
NAMEBOARD
RAMP
BO
PLATFORM
BOOKING HALL
WAITING ROOMS
URINAL
MILEPOST 7
OPEN DITCH
MILEPOST 0 + NOTICE
COTTAGE
LEVEL CROSSING
ASHES
OIL STORE
QUANTOCK TERRACE
STATION MASTER'S HOUSE
THE DROVE
From BRIDGWATER
BRISTOL ROAD

from EDINGTON JCN.
TRAMWAY
730 YDS
25 YDS
4
5. 6.
UP DOWN
8
9 7
7
11
8
14
12
246 YDS
10
13
10 YDS
WICKETS - 1.
GATE LOCK - 2.
Ground Level Frame.
Nº 3 Tablet to Edington Jcn.
Gates worked by hand.
SPARE : 3 :

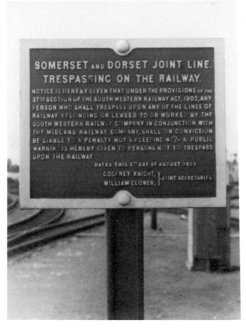

Appendix One

FACILITIES PROVIDED AT STATIONS OF THE SOMERSET & DORSET JOINT LINE
Railway Clearing House Handbook — 1938

Key:
G	—	Goods station
P	—	Passenger and Parcel station
p	—	Passenger, but not Parcel or Miscellaneous Traffic
F	—	Furniture Vans, Carriages, Motor Cars, Portable Engines and Machines on Wheels
L	—	Livestock
H	—	Horse Boxes and Prize Cattle Vans
C	—	Carriages and Motor Cars by Passenger Train
7-0	—	Capacity of fixed crane in tons and cwt

Stations

Bath Queen Square: G, P, F, L, H, C, 10-0
Midford: G, P, 7-0
Wellow: G, P, L, H
Shoscombe & Single Hill Halt: P
Radstock: G, P, L, H, 5-0
Midsomer Norton & Welton: G, P, F, L, H, C, 1-10
Chilcompton: G, P, F, L, H, C, 5-0
Binegar: G, P, L, H, 1-0
Masbury Halt: p
Shepton Mallet: G, P, F, L, H, C, 5-0
Evercreech New: G, P
Evercreech Junction: G, P, F, L, H, C, 1-0
Cole: G, P, F, L, H, C
Wincanton: G, P, F, L, H, 7-0
Templecombe (Lower): G, F, L
Templecombe (S & D part of Jnt station): P, H, C
Henstridge: G, P, F, L, H, C, 1-0
Stalbridge: G, P, F, L, H, C, 7-0
Sturminster Newton: G, P, F, L, H, C, 7-0
Shillingstone: G, P, F, L, H, C, 5-0
Stourpaine & Durweston Halt: p
Blandford: G, P, F, L, H, C, 7-0
Charlton Marshall Halt: p
Spetisbury Halt: p
Bailey Gate: G, P, F, L, H, C
Corfe Mullen Halt: p
Wimborne: G, P, F, L, H, C, 5-0
Broadstone: G, P, 5-0
Pylle: G, P, L, H, 1-10
West Pennard: G, P, L, H, C, 6-0
Glastonbury: G, P, F, L, H, C, 7-0
Ashcott: G, P
Shapwick: G, P, L, H
Edington Junction: G, P, L, H
Bason Bridge: G, P
Highbridge (S & D): G, P, F, L, H, C, 1-10
Highbridge (Wharf): G, L, 9-0
Burnham-on-Sea: G, P, F, H, C, 1-10
Cossington: G, P, F, L, H, C,
Bawdrip Halt: p
Bridgwater (S & D): G, P, F, L, H, C, 7-0
Polsham Halt: p
Polsham: G
Wells (S & D): G, P, F, L, H, C, 7-0

Appendix Two

PRIVATE SIDINGS AT SOMERSET AND DORSET JOINT LINE STATIONS

(Note: the sidings are listed under station as in the Handbook, regardless of possible actual location between stations.)
Railway Clearing House Handbook — 1938

Stations

BATH: Anglo-American Oil Co.'s
        Bath Gas Works
        Bonded Stores
        LMS Railway Co.'s Locomotive siding
        Shell-Mex and B.P. Ltd
        Stothert & Pitt

MIDFORD: Bath & Twerton Co-operative Society
          Victoria Brick & Tile Co.

WELLOW

RADSTOCK: Earl Waldegrave, Tyning's Colliery
            Foxcote Colliery
            Middle Pit Colliery
            Radstock Co-operative Industrial Society Ltd, Bakery siding
            Somersetshire Collieries Ltd, Braysdown Colliery
            Somersetshire Collieries Ltd, Ludlow Colliery
            Wagon Repairs Ltd
            Writhington Colliery

MIDSOMER NORTON: Norton Hill Colliery

CHILCOMPTON: New Rock Colliery
               Old Down (Emborough Stone Co. (1928) Ltd)

BINEGAR: Read & Sons

MASBURY: Emborough Stone Co. (1928) Ltd
          Roads Reconstruction (1934) Ltd

SHEPTON MALLET: Roads Reconstruction (1934) Ltd, Downside siding
                  Roads Reconstruction (1934) Ltd, Hamwood siding
                  Roads Reconstruction (1934) Ltd, Winsor Hill siding

EVERCREECH NEW: Evercreech Lime & Sone Co.

EVERCREECH JUNCTION: C & T Harris & Co. Ltd.
                      Somerset Brick & Tile Co.

COLE:

WINCANTON: Cow & Gate Ltd
             Dried Milk Products Ltd
             F.G. Minter Ltd

TEMPLECOMBE:

HENSTRIDGE:

STALBRIDGE:

STURMINSTER NEWTON: Milk Marketing Board

SHILLINGSTONE:

BLANDFORD:

BAILEY GATE: Carter's siding
               Royal Naval Pumping Station
               United Dairy Co.

PYLLE:

WEST PENNARD:

GLASTONBURY: Snow & Co.

ASHCOTT: Eclipse Peat Co.
          Petfu siding

SHAPWICK:

EDINGTON JUNCTION:

BASON BRIDGE: Wilts. United Dairies Co.

HIGHBRIDGE: Bland & Co.'s timber yard
              Highbridge Trading Co.
              Willett's Cake Mills

BURNHAM-ON-SEA: Colthurst, Symons & Co. Ltd, Brick siding

COSSINGTON:

BRIDGWATER: Board's siding
             Wharf

POLSHAM:

WELLS:

Other sidings on the line (not previously illustrated).

WILD'S CEMENT WORKS

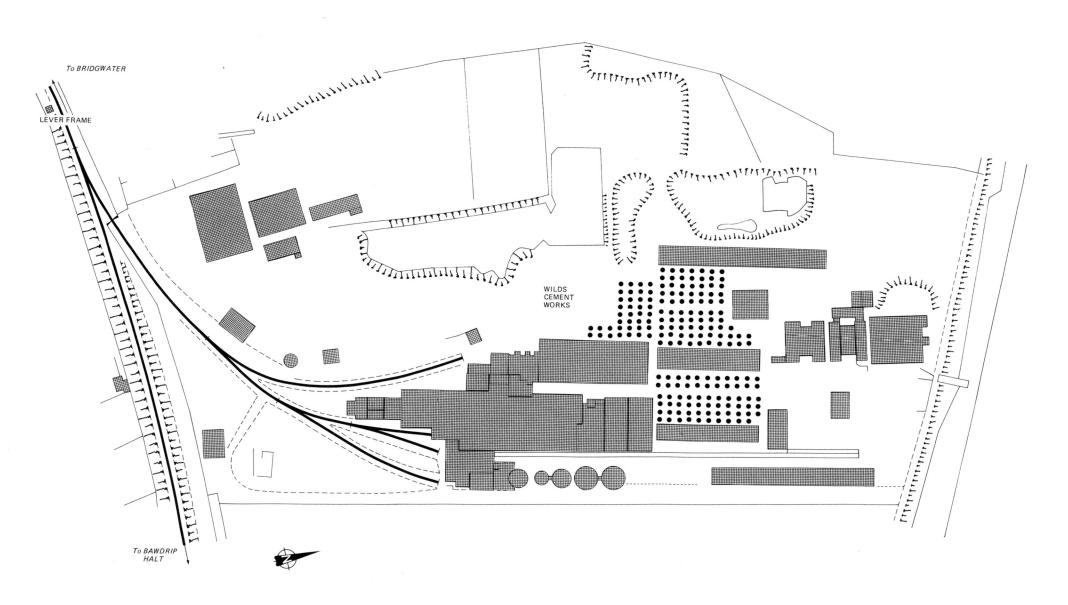

To BRIDGWATER

LEVER FRAME

WILDS
CEMENT
WORKS

To BAWDRIP
HALT

APEX & COLTHURST, SYMONS SIDINGS

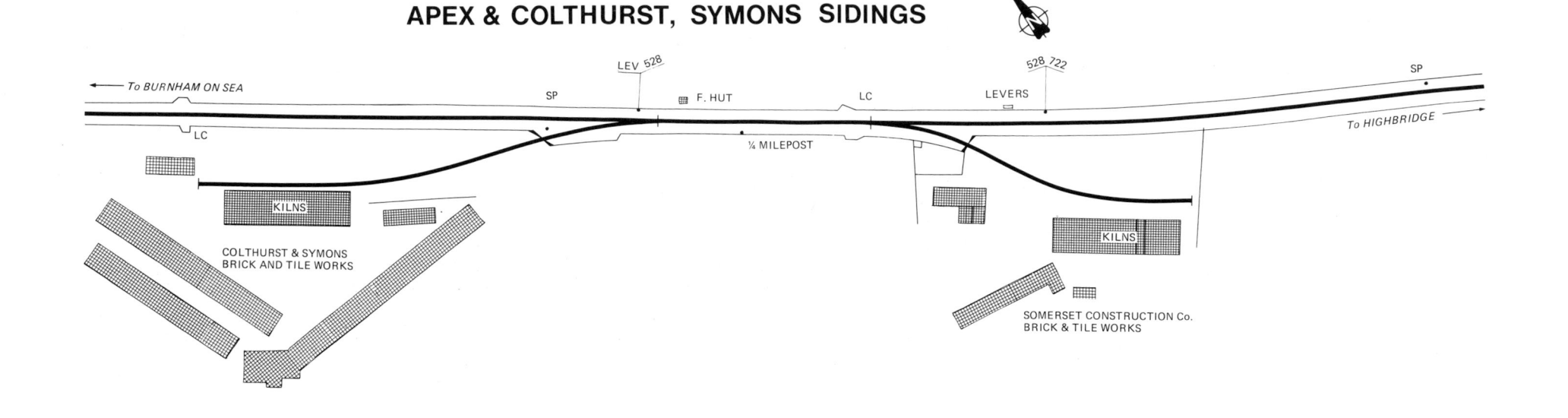

← To BURNHAM ON SEA

SP

LEV 528

F. HUT

LC

528 722

LEVERS

SP

LC

To HIGHBRIDGE

¼ MILEPOST

KILNS

COLTHURST & SYMONS
BRICK AND TILE WORKS

KILNS

SOMERSET CONSTRUCTION Co.
BRICK & TILE WORKS

BOARDS SIDING

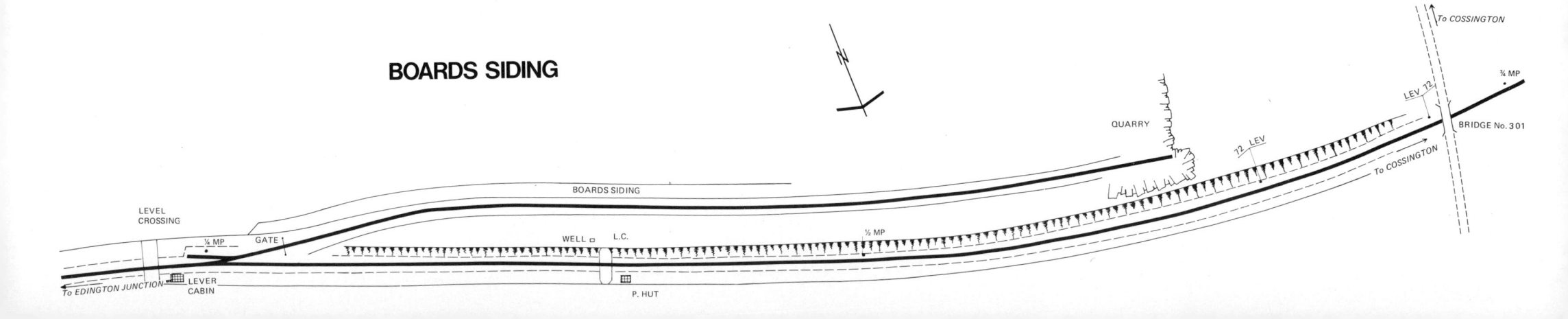

To COSSINGTON

¾ MP

QUARRY

LEV 72

BRIDGE No. 301

72 LEV

To COSSINGTON

BOARDS SIDING

LEVEL
CROSSING

¼ MP

GATE

WELL

L.C.

½ MP

To EDINGTON JUNCTION

LEVER
CABIN

P. HUT

The End